THE BACKWARD TRAIL

Stories of the Indians and Tennessee Pioneers

BY

WILL T. HALE

Author of " In an Autumn Lane, and Other Poems and Dialect Pieces"

NASHVILLE, TENN.
THE CUMBERLAND PRESS
1899

Notice

In many older books, foxing (or discoloration) occurs and, in some instances, print lightens with wear and age. Reprinted books, such as this, often duplicate these flaws, notwithstanding efforts to reduce or eliminate them. The pages of this reprint have been digitally enhanced and, where possible, the flaws eliminated in order to provide clarity of content and a pleasant reading experience.

Copyright © 1899, by Will T. Hale

Originally published
Nashville, Tennessee:
1899

Reprinted by:

Janaway Publishing, Inc.
2412 Nicklaus Dr.
Santa Maria, California 93455
(805) 925-1038
www.janawaygenealogy.com

2009, 2012

ISBN 13: 978-1-59641-180-7

Made in the United States of America

INTRODUCTION.

In seeking to present the strange and romantic, the thrilling and marvelous, we need not indulge the imagination. The history of Tennessee abounds in facts stranger than fiction.

Speaking of the various deeds of the Savior while on earth, Saint John avers: "If they should be written every one, I suppose that even the world could not contain the books that should be written." Many volumes could be profitably and interestingly filled with heroic acts of our ancestors. In presenting the following, the object has been to give precedence to only a few of the salient occurrences, and to try to treat them in such a manner as will stimulate the study of our annals by the young. The truth has been adhered to throughout so far as the author was able to discern it.

The author acknowledges his obligations for valuable assistance rendered him by Dr. R. L. C. White, the eminent specialist in Tennessee history.

CONTENTS.

CHAPTER I.
A Glance at Tennessee's Progress, and Reviewing Some of Its Landmarks.................................. 2

CHAPTER II.
The Earliest Discovery of Tennessee Soil, and the Destruction of Old Fort Loudoun.................. 13

CHAPTER III.
The Watauga Association, with an Account of an Attempt to Destroy the First Settlements......... 23

CHAPTER IV.
John Sevier, Soldier and Statesman, as well as a Notice of the State of Franklin 32

CHAPTER V.
The Settling of Middle Tennessee, noting the Beginning of Indian Atrocities 44

CHAPTER VI.
Further Mention of Events in the Cumberland Settlements, and James Robertson's Achievements...... 50

CHAPTER VII.
An Interesting Record, Together with a Tragedy on Stone's River.................................... 67

CHAPTER VIII.
Territorial Matters, Including Some of the Public Acts of William Blount................................. 82

CONTENTS.

CHAPTER IX.
The Nickojack Expedition, Which Resulted in Breaking the Spirit of the Indians...... 94

CHAPTER X.
Mere Glimpses of Certain Other Characters Figuring in the Earlier Settlements...... 102

CHAPTER XI.
Endurance and Heroism of Frontier Women, and Some Instances Particularized...... 120

CHAPTER XII.
The Pastimes of the Settlers, and Their Whole-souled Hospitality...... 130

CHAPTER XIII.
Early Religious Sentiment, and the Faithful Work of the Ministers...... 136

CHAPTER XIV.
The Tribes Claiming a Right to Lands at the First Settlement, and Their Present Status...... 144

CHAPTER XV.
The Mound Builders or Stone Grave Race, and Some Archæological Researches...... 154

CHAPTER XVI.
The Battle of King's Mountain, and Tennessee's Connection with the Revolution...... 164

CHAPTER XVII.
The Story of Constitution Making, from the Watauga Association to 1800...... 171

CHAPTER I.

A GLANCE AT TENNESSEE'S PROGRESS, AND REVIEWING SOME OF ITS LANDMARKS.

Tennessee was admitted into the Union on May 31, or June 1, 1796, the third State coming in under the Federal constitution, although in 1794 it had become a distinct territorial government. The seat of government was at Knoxville from 1794 to 1811, excepting for a short period only in 1807, when it was at Kingston; from 1812 to 1815 it was at Nashville; in 1817 it was again removed to Knoxville, and from there in 1819 to Murfreesboro, where it remained until 1826; then Nashville became the capital. The State is bounded north by Kentucky and Virginia, southeast by North Carolina, south by Georgia, Alabama, Mississippi, and west by Arkansas and Missouri. Its population was 35,691 in 1790, and 1,767,518 about a century later. The largest cities are Nashville, Knoxville, Memphis and Chattanooga; and the governors of the State, not including the territorial governor, William Blount, have been: John Sevier, 1796; Archibald Roane, 1801; John Sevier, 1803; Willie Blount, 1809; Joseph McMinn, 1815; William Carroll, 1821; Samuel

Houston, 1827—resigned April 16, 1829, and was succeeded by William Hall, Speaker of the Senate; William Carroll, 1829; Newton Cannon, 1835; James K. Polk, 1839; James C. Jones, 1841; Aaron V. Brown, 1845; Neill S. Brown, 1847; William Trousdale, 1849; William B. Campbell, 1851; Andrew Johnson, 1853; Isham G. Harris, 1857; Andrew Johnson, military governor by appointment from 1862 to 1865; William G. Brownlow, 1865—resigned February 25, 1869, and was succeeded by D.W. C. Senter, Speaker of the Senate; D. W. C. Senter, 1869: John C. Brown, 1871; James D. Porter, 1875; Albert S. Marks, 1879; Alvin Hawkins, 1881; William B. Bate, 1883; Robert L. Taylor, 1887; John P. Buchanan, 1891; Peter Turney, 1893; Robert L. Taylor, 1897; Benton McMillin, 1899.

The climate is generally mild and salubrious, excepting in the more swampy districts of the western portion of the State, and assures a great variety of vegetable productions. Several indigenous grasses spring spontaneously; black and red haws, woodgrapes, wild plums, black, whortle and goose berries, hickorynuts, chestnuts, walnuts, pecans and chinquapins, all grow in abundance; so that it can be readily seen that it must have seemed a delightful land for a home by those hunters and explorers who occasionally passed through some portions before emigration was actually turned to the western country.

Tennessee has made rapid strides within a century, and is now one of the most progressive of the Southern

A VAST WILDERNESS.

States. When we consider its present development, it is almost impossible to believe that before the year 1750 it was a vast wilderness, uninhabited by any white person. Where beautiful towns and cities now flourish and elegant rural homes are situated, then buffalos bellowed and fought around the salt licks, bears passed through the cane and underbrush, deer stalked down to the streams to slake their thirst, panthers screamed from their coverts, and the wild turkeys called to each other in the solitude.

Now and then adventurous explorers passed down the larger streams, returning to the colonies with wonderful tales of the wilderness, and occasionally bands of Indians ventured into the fastnesses, to go back to their villages after a few weeks laden with game; but no white man dared to make the Tennessee region his home before the middle of the eighteenth century, and even the savages laid no serious claim to much of it as a part of their domains.

Taming the wilderness now is an easy and pleasant task, with railroads and other facilities for traveling, not to mention the ease with which the settler can get the other requirements for his work of home-making. But when the first settlers came to Tennessee, the journey was a long and perilous undertaking, and the first years' struggles were often sufficient to depress strong hearts. A historian has recently described the founding of new settlements in graphic language. As a rule, he says, the settlers came in groups for mutual protection, and perhaps for mutual encouragement. The household goods were borne on the backs of horses, called pack-horses, and consisted generally of a few cooking utensils, a wooden trencher for kneading dough, several small packages containing salt and some seed corn, a flask or two of medicine, wearing apparel, a wife, and sometimes a baby at the breast. Their daughters walked beside the mother on the horse and the sons were with the fathers a few paces in front. If a cow and a few pigs were added to their outfit the future founders of the commonwealth regarded their lot as peculiarly fortunate.

Having arrived at the place of destination, they set to work to erect a cabin, a primitive affair of logs, with a top of clapboards held in place by weights. The furniture consisted of a bedstead, a washstand, a few three-legged stools, a table, a water bucket, a gourd dipper, and pegs about the walls for hanging clothes, rifles, game and the like. The chief covering for the family in cold weather was rarely a blanket, often the skins of deer and bear, and occasionally buffalo, tanned so as to be soft and supple. The fare consisted of game, which was abundant and delicate. Bread was made of corn, beaten as fine as possible in an improvised mortar. It was made into dough on a trencher and baked in the ashes and called ash-cake, or baked before the fire and called Johnny-cake, a corruption from Journey-cake, from the ease with which it could be made. The corn itself could also be made into mush, and where the cow had prospered, mush and milk made the favorite diet, for supper especially. A delicious syrup was gotten from the maple. Butter was supplied from the fat of bear's meat, or the gravy of the goose. Coffee was made from parched rye and dried beans. Tea was supplied by the sassafras tree. The location of the cabin was as near to a spring as possible. The garden was laid off not far from the cabin. All trees within gunshot of the house, large enough to conceal the body of an Indian, were carefully cut down. A shed was built in the yard for the horses and pigs, which were allowed to run at large during times of peace, to grow fat upon the mast, and trained to return at eventide and seek shelter from wolves and the depredations of bears.

A few of the cabins and better class of habitations of the earlier days are standing yet—battered urns whose dust was scattered long ago. Near the main road leading to Sevierville, and about five miles from Knoxville, in a deserted and worn-out field, are the ruins of an old log station. During the war between John Sevier and his comrades against the Cherokees for the protection of the French Broad settlers, the place became the refuge of a number of families, and it had been a frontier post before Knoxville was settled. The land around it was bought by Gen. Sevier, the great Indian fighter, about 1790. He added to the buildings, and even after he was Governor of Tennessee lived there in rustic simplicity. He kept open house and entertained his friends and guests, who were numerous. Among his visitors often were the Indian chiefs, John Watts, Double Head and Bloody Fellow, who, as the historian observes, came to stretch their moccasins before the great wood fire, or eat of Sevier's venison, or ask his advice on the important affairs of their nation.

A few miles east of Nashville, not far from the Hermitage, the first dwelling of Andrew Jackson may be seen, gray and dilapidated. It is also a log structure, of three rooms and a capacious fire-place that looks as if it might chamber a quarter of a cord of wood. Rude as this building is, it once sheltered many a distinguished person, among them Aaron Burr, the fastidious New York statesman. The visitor to the landmark, by a very slight effort of the imagination, can hear old voices in the gloom, recall evenings when Jackson and his wife—lovers from marriage until separation by death—sat by the door and talked of their future plans, the whippoorwill in the woods

"Threshing the summer dusk
With his gold flail of song,"

and the insects in the undergrowth making the evening sweet with a thousand toned delights.

Another building having an interest because of its age if for nothing else may be seen some sixty miles east of Nashville—the Overall homestead, in DeKalb County. It is situated upon the western bank of a beautiful stream, not more than two miles from the crossing at the Buffalo Ford on the Indian trail which led from the Cumberland Mountains to the early settlements on the Cumberland river, and near the Nashville and Knoxville turnpike. Its present owner was born there about 1830, was a number of times a member of the Legislature, and has many interesting things to tell of the homestead and its first possessor. "My father purchased the place about the year 1800," he will tell you. "Of course you see I have remodeled the building somewhat, but the portion that was standing when he became owner is still intact. The first settler here was a man named Looney, who was not held in high esteem by the few settlers hereabouts, for he was thought to have made his property by unfair means, and was in addition supposed to be too much in sympathy with Indians. My father came from Virginia, bringing his stock and negroes with him; and you may wonder at it, but I have now the same breed of dun cattle that were brought here soon after the territory became the State of Tennessee. And," he will continue, with a twinkle of humor in his blue eyes, "I have lived in three counties, though I was born in this house and never moved in my life. The farm was first in Smith County; when Cannon was made from a portion of Smith, I found myself in Cannon. The plantation is now in the county of DeKalb. On Smith Fork creek, at the Buffalo Ford, there occurred the fight with the Indians which is recorded in Carr's Tennessee history. The spot is just above the present ford, a mile north of my farm, and by looking at the place and reflecting that it was then covered with cane and heavy undergrowth, a person need not wonder that the Indians made a good stand. Gen. Winchester, of the Sumner County settlements, while out upon a scouting expedition, came upon fresh traces of Indians. He and his party pursued them down what is now known as Smith Fork creek until reaching the ford. He saw there that the Indians had decided to stop and give battle. His spies—two of them—were in front. When they entered the canebrake a short distance, the savages, lying in ambush, fired upon them. The spy named Hickerson was killed. Gen. Winchester and his force hurried up, and the battle lasted some time. But the Indians had the advantage in numbers and position, and the former were forced to withdraw. Capt. James McCann killed an Indian on this occasion who was supposed to be a celebrated chief and warrior known as the Moon, as he was hare-lipped, and it was claimed that there was but one hare-lipped man in the tribe to which the body of Indians belonged.

"Speaking further of the Indians, many of them came through Cannon County when migrating beyond the Mississippi river. My father visited their camps, as did many of the farmers. He said that he was able, after seeing them on the way from their old hunting grounds and the graves of their fathers, to form a better idea of the appearance of the Hebrews when leaving Egypt. Many of them were wealthy, having their slaves and fine horses.

"I have heard my parents speak of their early days here. They were often uneasy over thoughts of Indian violence, though no massacre took place. There were alarms now and then, when the neighbors would all go to one house and remain until the scare was over. As late as 1865-66 it was not an uncommon occurrence for a few Indians to leave the fastnesses of North Carolina or East Tennessee and pass through this section on a wearisome journey to the far West."

Finally: The Goodpasture house still stands on Buffalo creek, near Hillham, in Overton County. It is a large two-story log structure, with only one door in the front and one window in the upper story. It was erected in 1800, while the country between Livingston (now the county seat of Overton County), and Kingston, then a federal fort at the junction of Holston and Clinch rivers, was occupied by the Cherokee Indians. This section is now known as the "mountain district" of the State. It is a romantic country, and the facts concerning its early settlement are full of interest. It extends northwestwardly, between the Cumberland Mountains and the Cumberland and Caney Fork rivers, from a line drawn lengthwise through the centre of the State to the Kentucky line, embracing the present counties of Overton, White, Jackson, Putnam, Fentress, Clay and Pickett. All of it was not opened for settlement at the same time. By the treaty of Holston, in 1791, the Indian line began at a point on Cumberland river, from which a southwest line would strike the ridge that divides the waters of Cumberland from those of Duck river, forty miles above Nashville. The line ran two and a half miles east of Livingston, dividing the district into two almost equal parts. The West was open to settlement, and the East (known as the Wilderness) reserved to the Cherokees. By an act of the General Assembly in 1798, the line of the Indian reservation was made the eastern boundary of Sumner County, which, in 1799, was reduced to its constitutional limits, and the new counties of Smith and Wilson established out of its former territory. Two years later Smith County was reduced, and Jackson County established, extending to the Wilderness. By the treaty of Tellico, in 1805, the Indian title to the Wilderness was extinguished, and the entire mountain district opened. In this part of the State are Obeds and Roaring rivers, and on the banks of the latter the Long Hunters spent eight or nine months of the years 1769-70 while exploring the West. The Goodpasture family came from Kingston by the Walton road—which was then marked out between that place to the present village of Carthage, and completed in 1801. "The road," say A. V. and W. H. Goodpasture in a biographical and historical work, "was about a hundred miles in length, and contained four stands for the accommodation of travelers. Coming West, the first of these was at Kimbrough's, on the eastern foot of the mountain; the second at Crab Orchard, a once famous place on the mountain plateau, in Cumberland County; the third at White's Plain, in Putnam County, on the western foot of the mountain; and the fourth near Pekin, also in Putnam County." There were few settlers there at the time; Indians were now and then seen, and buffalo were still to be found; but a few years later settlers came from Virginia, Pennsylvania and East Tennessee, among them the widow and some of the children of the great Indian fighter and first governor of Tennessee, Gen. John Sevier. In time there also came the ancestors of Samuel L. Clemens ("Mark Twain"), the most popular humorist in the world, locating at Jamestown, Fentress County.

The landmarks mentioned are rife with memories. There were tears and laughter, love and hate, hope and despair, and all the vicissitudes and changes that are the heritage of mankind. We can see the sturdy husbandman as he goes about his labors to tame the wild country, and the housewife blithely doing the duties allotted to her; neighbors enjoying each other's companionship with greater pleasure because so rare, and the young people, as the Indian youths and maidens before them, experiencing love's young dream, their souls radiant in the light that never was on land or sea; revolutionary veterans who had seen service at Valley Forge or the Cowpens or along the Brandywine, now entitled to somewhat of rest, fishing in the beautiful streams, making wolf traps, or hunting the turkey for pastime. And those log walls, still intact after the forms that held immortal souls have fallen to dust, serve to recall Dobson's lines on the Pompadour's fan:

> "Where are the secrets it knew?
> Weavings of plot and of plan?
> But where is the Pompadour, too?
> *This* was the Pompadour's *fan!*"

CHAPTER II.

THE EARLIEST DISCOVERY OF TENNESSEE SOIL, AND THE DESTRUCTION OF OLD FORT LOUDOUN.

It is an interesting tradition that Ferdinand De Soto, a Spanish explorer, first discovered the magnificent country now known as Tennessee more than two centuries before its first settlement. Fired by the idea of conquest and urged by the hope of finding gold in the New World, he sailed from Havana May 12, 1539, with an army of about one thousand men, besides the marines. There were also three hundred and fifty horses. He passed through the domains of a number of Indian rulers, meeting with considerable opposition, and finally reached the eastern border of Tennessee. Keeping a western course, he arrived, in April, 1541, in sight of the Indian village, Chisca, supposed to be the present site of Memphis. According to Irving, the Indians of this province knew nothing of the approach of the strangers until the latter rushed in upon them, taking many prisoners and pillaging the houses. De Soto remained in the town some twenty days, and having had four floats constructed, crossed the Mississippi river at a point known as the Chickasaw Bluffs, and passed with his band of adventurers to the failure that awaited his aspirations and dreams. More than a century later, La Salle, passing down the Mississippi, built a fort called Prud'homme, near Memphis, in 1714 the French built the successor of Prud'homme, calling it Fort Assumption, and still later Fort San Ferdinando de Barancas was erected by the Spanish government at the mouth of Wolf river in the hope of building the Southwestern Empire of North America. When the United States came into possession of the Mississippi Valley, the fort was taken possession of by the Americans and dismantled, while Fort Pickering was built further down the river.

It is thus seen that the western section of the State was early discovered. But it was the last to be opened up to civilization, the treaty of 1818, by which the Chickasaw Indians relinquished their rights to Tennessee, being the beginning of its history. Memphis, the metropolis of that section, had its birth in the early part of 1819. The virgin wilderness around it at that time, Phelan says, bore scarcely a trace of the human hand; the foundations of both city and county were laid under the shadows and around the roots of trees in the midst of tangled undergrowth. The old blockhouse still stood in Fort Pickering and a few straggling shanties clustered around a large and primitive structure known as the public warehouse, sometimes called Young's warehouse, in the neighborhood of Wolf river. Between these two were thick cane-brakes and a heavy and luxuriant growth of timber, through which a narrow footpath ran from Fort Pickering to Wolf river. The growth into importance of the city has been marvelous. Though founded after Nashville and Knoxville had acquired size and reputation, it is now hardly rivaled in the Southwest, from a commercial standpoint. A city of beauty and prosperity, it stands above the Father of Waters, interesting as its namesake on the Nile when at its best. In its midst bud and bloom the flowers of a semi-tropic clime; the fragrance of the garden of Gul permeates its residence streets; along its business throughfares the baled snow of the cottonfields of Mississippi, Arkansas and West Tennessee is drawn, promising warmth and comfort for the world's millions. The entire western section has developed also, until one, considering it, recalls the tribute a Southern singer has paid the South: "No fairer land hath fired a poet's lays, or given a home to man."

Despite the early discovery of the western borders, and the fact that the Chickasaw Bluffs have played an important part in the political history of Spain, France and England, the first actual settlements were made in the East; though the home of the Chickasaw Indians, West Tennessee was not the arena in which the blood of the pioneers was spilled to make a commonwealth. The Watauga neighborhood is given as the scene of the first settlement; but it is not venturing too much to say that had Fort Loudoun escaped destruction in 1760, that would have been the point from which colonization would have spread. The old fort has a pathetic interest, and has been considered of sufficient importance to induce Miss Murfree, a leading American fictionist, to make it the subject of one of her latest novels.

The fort was built in 1757 on the Tennessee river about thirty miles from the present city of Knoxville, and a mile above the mouth of the Tellico. It and another had been erected by the British in the Cherokee territory with the consent of the Indians, for protection against the French and their allies, and was one hundred and fifty miles west of the nearest white settlement. Garrisoned by about two hundred British regulars, the traders, hunters and a few settlers soon made the place the centre of a thriving settlement.

While the tragedy of Fort Loudoun excites our horror, the Indians had great provocation. In many instances the whites had treated them as though the Indians had no rights that should be respected, and as if independence were a thing to be monopolized by the Anglo-Americans. For instance, the first man who was known to have resided among the Cherokees—the destroyers of the fort in question—was Cornelius Dougherty, an Irishman who established himself as a trader among them in 1690. He introduced horses among them, and they soon began stealing the animals from the whites. In retaliation, the whites, living along the seacoast of Carolina, encouraged the tribes living nearer the Atlantic to steal the Cherokees themselves. Hundreds of the latter were captured, sold to the colonists, and by them consigned to hard labor in the malarial swamps, or shipped to Cuba.

The cause which brought about the massacre of the Fort Loudoun garrison reflects no credit on the whites. The British and French were at war with each other, and the Cherokees assisted the former. The Indians lost their horses during the expedition, and on returning through Western Virginia to their homes, after the capture of Fort Du Quesne, they appropriated a number of horses which they found running in the woods. With an ingratitude that was never exceeded by the Indians themselves, the German settlers of that region attacked the unsuspecting Indians in the night, and killed and scalped fourteen. They also took a number of prisoners. It is stated that these ingrates, who forgot that the Cherokees had assisted in protecting their homes from the French, imposed the scalps they took on the government for those of French Indians, and obtained the premium allowed at that time by law. This naturally aroused a deep resentment, and Oconostota, head king or archimagus of the Cherokees, set about to seek swift and bloody revenge.

The Cherokees at once deserted the English and began their massacres. Gov. W. H. Littleton, of South Carolina, made preparation to force them into repentance and submission. He levied a considerable army. Awed, and designing, probably, to gain an advantage, the savages sent commissioners to treat with Littleton. He ordered them into the rear of the army. After arriving at Fort St. George, the commissioners, twenty-one chiefs, were held as prisoners there, the Indians agreeing to their retention until an equal number of those who had slain the inhabitants on the frontiers should be given up in exchange for them.

Atta-Kulla-Kulla, vice-king, was a party to this agreement, but desired that some of the chiefs who were imprisoned might be liberated to assist him in placating the Indians. Oconostota and two other chiefs were given up, while other Indians were taken in exchange.

These twenty-one hostages remained in prison about two months, when the Cherokees resolved to attempt their liberation by stratagem. The army had just left the country, and on February 16, 1760, two Indian women appeared at Keowee, on the opposite bank of the river, no doubt to assist in carrying out some scheme of Oconostota. An officer of the garrison went out and began talking with them. Presently Oconostota came up. He drew from the fort two other officers to converse with him, declaring that he wanted a white man to go with him to have a talk with Gov. Littleton; among these officers was Capt. Cotymore, against whom the head chief entertained a deep-rooted hatred. By some means a plan seemed to have been concerted between the hostages and the Indians without—for it was soon shown that a body of savages were in hiding near where he and the whites were talking.

A FORT ATTACKED. 19

When promised a guard to go with him to Charleston, the chief, who held a bridle in his hand, said he would go and catch his horse. Then quickly turning himself about, he swung his bridle three times over his head. This was a signal, and immediately about thirty guns were discharged at the group of officers. Cotymore received a fatal wound, and the other officers, Lieutenants Foster and Bell, were wounded. They were enabled to reach the fort with Capt. Cotymore, and ordered the hostages put in irons. An Englishman laid hold of one of them, and was stabbed to death, and in the scuffle which now took place two or three other whites were wounded and driven from the place of confinement. The affair was by this time beginning to look serious.

The attacking Indians were yelling outside, while the hostages were shouting to encourage their friends and making every possible effort to prevent being shackled by the British.

The fort proved too strong for Oconostota's primitive methods, and successfully resisted his siege. Infuriated at the treachery of the Indians and the bloody resistance of the hostages, the whites committed a piece of brutality that may be justifiable in contending with savages, but a thoughtful public will doubt the exigency; they cut a hole in the roof of the room in which the Indian prisoners were confined, and shooting down, butchered the entire number!

The war soon began to rage in all its horrors. Gathering a large force of Cherokee braves, Oconostota and Atta-Kulla-Kulla invested Fort Loudoun. They had on March 3 assaulted with musketry the fort at Ninety-six, with no effect, and had met Col. Montgomery and his force near their village at Etchoe, and, according to Haywood, "treated him so rudely that, though he claimed the victory, he retreated to Fort St. George, whence he shortly afterward went to New York." They were to meet with a measure of success at Fort Loudoun.

They besieged this place for weeks. Provisions became so scarce that the whites were compelled to eat horses and dogs. In vain did the little garrison look for Col. Montgomery or for any other succor. Englishmen were defending—and the stubbornness of the defense can be imagined; each soldier could say, as those who later defended Lucknow:

"Handful of men as we were, we were English in heart
 and in limb,
 Strong with the strength of the race to command, to
 obey, to endure;
Each of us fought as if hope for the garrison hung but
 on him;
 Still—could we watch at all points? we were every day
 fewer and fewer."

Finally the savages agreed to terms; the whites were to be allowed a safe retreat to the settlements beyond the Blue Ridge. The latter on August 7, 1760, threw into the river their cannon and buried a quantity of ammunition, and taking with them such small arms as were necessary for hunting, began their march to South Carolina settlements. A number of Indians accompanied them, ostensibly as guards.

They traveled unmolested for about twenty miles. Hope began to rise exultant again—the savages seemed to be keeping faith. But toward evening the Indian guard disappeared in the wilderness. Reaching a place afterwards called Katy Harlin's Reserve, they camped. Never, perhaps, to these three or four hundred whites just out of the mouth of hell had the mocking-bird's song in the woods sounded more cheerful; never had the sun gone down in more gorgeous beauty; never had the insects made evening more sweetly musical.

The night passed without event, but about daybreak there was a yell of savages and the report of fire-arms. Many of the whites were killed at the first volley, while the Cherokees rushed into the camp, destroying, as one chronicler has it, the entire party—men, women and children—except three men who were saved by the friendly exertions of Atta-Kulla-Kulla, and also six others who had gone on ahead as advance guard. Among those captured was Stuart, a friend of Atta-Kulla-Kulla, who afterwards, as agent to the Southern Indians, incited them to take part with England in our war for independence, and to attempt the massacre of the entire white settlements of Western North Carolina.

Between two and three hundred men, besides women and children, fell in this slaughter. The Indians made a fence of their bones. For years thereafter the place was shunned as a spot accursed. Emigration along that route ceased, and, unmolested, the wolves hovered near and the vultures wheeled above the veritable Place of Skulls.

In the summer of 1761 the Cherokees were forced to sue for peace after their towns had been burned, their cornfields laid waste and their stock slaughtered or driven away by the avenging whites.

CHAPTER III.

THE WATAUGA ASSOCIATION, WITH AN ACCOUNT OF AN ATTEMPT TO DESTROY THE FIRST SETTLEMENTS.

"East Tennessee began to be permanently settled in the winter of 1768-69," says Haywood. "Ten families of these settlers came from the neighborhood of the place where Raleigh now stands, in North Carolina, and settled on the Watauga. This was the first settlement in East Tennessee."

Capt. William Bean came from Virginia in 1769, built a cabin on the Watauga, near the mouth of Boone's creek, and his son, Russell, was the first white child born in Tennessee. But the small settlement in the wilderness was added to by other settlers every month, and by 1772 Watauga was quite a flourishing community. Among these later arrivals should be mentioned James Robertson, especially since he was to become so prominently connected with affairs, first at Watauga and later on the Cumberland. He came to Watauga in 1770, but not making the settlement his home until 1771.

Phelan properly says that the settlements along the Watauga were made at a time peculiarly fortunate; the Indian warfare had exterminated nearly all of the Indian race in the neighborhood; the Shawnees existed only in small, wandering detatchments, and were generally hidden away in the lofty recesses of the Cumberland Mountains; the Creeks of the Cumberland region had been massacred by the Cherokees, and the latter, emboldened by continued success, had invaded the Chickasaws and been repulsed with terrible slaughter. For the time being, and until the Cherokees had recuperated sufficiently to make war on the whites, the chief danger arose from bands of marauding Indians.

Other settlements sprung up in the meantime—that in Carter's Valley, in the neighborhood of where Rogersville now is, and that on the Nollichucky, its prime mover being Jacob Brown, who opened a store. Forts were built at these places for their protection.

There is much confusion in the history of the earlier settlement of the eastern section up to 1772. There had sprung up communities in Carter's Valley and on the Nollichucky; the settlers had been seriously puzzled as to whether they belonged to Virginia or North Carolina, and the Watauga people at last resolved to form an association for their own protection. Phelan says that at first only two original settlements lived under the articles—presumably Watauga and Carter's Valley, for, he says further, that in 1775 the Brown or Nollichucky pioneers, being composed mostly of Tories, were compelled to take the oath to the Colonial cause in the war with Great Britain by the

The Watauga Association. 25

Wataugans and a band of Virginians from Wolf's Hill, and from that time on became identified with those who framed the articles of association. Roosevelt, Bancroft, Ramsey and other writers appear somewhat confused on this point, as they do on the mode of government of Watauga. But it seems clear that the association was formed in 1772, and that the settlers lived under it—virtually in an independent colony—until attached to North Carolina.

Mere speculation on these points is foreign to this work, for like the silliness called higher criticism of the Bible, it tends only to confuse; and the rewards of so much contention seem hardly worth while.

In 1776 the population of the three settlements was estimated at six hundred, and about that time they gave their section the name of Washington District, and petitioned to be annexed to North Carolina. Their petition was accepted, and the first independent government on Tennessee soil came to an end. It was to be followed in a few years by that of the government of Franklin, also to collapse before the machinery of the State of Tennessee was to be put into regular motion.

The residents of Washington District had declared themselves in favor of the cause for American independence, and their patriotism came near proving their extinction. In 1776 they were suddenly warned of an impending outbreak by the Indians. One Cameron, under the direction of John Stuart, who had been saved from death in the Fort Loudoun affair by Atta-Kulla-Kulla, assembled the chiefs of the Cherokees and bribed them to attack the district, to destroy its inhabitants to a man, and then invade Virginia and North and South Carolina. It is unnecessary to say that the people were horrified over the news. They were acquainted with Indian warfare, its horrors, its mercilessness. Backed by England, what might not the savages accomplish?

Seven hundred warriors were to make the attack in two divisions, each division to attack one of the two strongest forts, Watauga and Heaton. This scheme was divulged to the whites by Nancy Ward, a friendly Indian woman.

The forts were strengthened and provisioned, and runners were sent through the settlements to give the people warning and to tell them to repair at once to the forts. Five small companies, raised partly in Virginia, assembled, the oldest officer being Capt. Thompson. They marched to Heaton's station. There they remained for a day or two, when it was learned that the Indians, in a body of three or four hundred, were actually approaching. Just above the fort were flat lands, with a few bushes and saplings, but otherwise open; it was decided by the whites to go out and meet the enemy on the flats. The corps consisted of one hundred and seventy men, with an advance of ten or twelve troops in front. Reaching the flats, the advance discovered a small party of Indians and drove them back, but did not meet the main body. A halt was made and a council was held by the whites, the conclusion being that they would probably not meet the savages that day, and it would be prudent to return to the fort. During the consultation, and while the soldiers were formed in line, some one made an unfavorable remark relative to the lack of courage of one of the captains. "He soon heard of it," says Haywood, "and the corps having commenced its returning march in the same order as they had marched forward, the captain whom the remark implicated, being at the head of the right line, after going a short distance, halted, and addressed the troops in defense of himself against the imputation. The whole body collected into a crowd to hear him. After the address was over the offended captain took the head of his line, marching on the road that led to the station. But before all the troops had fallen into the ranks, and left the place where they had halted, it was announced that the Indians were advancing in order of battle in the rear! Capt. Thompson, the senior officer, who on the returning march was at the head of the left line, ordered the right line to form for battle to the right, and the line which he headed to the left, and to face the enemy. In attempting to form the line the head of the right seemed to bear too much along the road leading to the station, and the part of the line farther back, perceiving that the Indians were endeavoring to outflank them, were drawn off by Lieut. Robert Davis as quickly as possible, and formed on the right, across the flat to a ridge, and prevented them from getting around the flank. This movement of Lieut. Davis cut off a part of the right line, which had kept too far along the road. Some of them, however, when the firing began, returned to the main body, which was drawn up in order of battle, and a few of them kept on to the station. The greater part of the officers, and not a few of the privates, gave heroic examples to cause the men to face about and give battle. Of the latter Robert Edmiston and John Morrison made conspicuous exertions. They advanced some paces toward the enemy, and began the battle by shooting down the foremost."

The chief who led the Indians was Dragging Canoe. His warriors began the attack with great fury, the foremost yelling: "The Unacas are running; come on and scalp them!" Their first effort was to break through the centre of Thompson's command and then crush his flanks in detail. But they were not used to direct fire, and after a few volleys fled, leaving twenty-six warriors dead. The wounded of the savages died till the whole loss amounted to about forty. Not a white man was killed, and only five wounded, who subsequently recovered. This battle took place in July, 1776.

Hand to hand conflicts were not uncommon in those times. One which took place in the battle on the flats is recorded. A soldier named Moore had shot a chief,

HAND-TO-HAND CONFLICT. 29

wounding him in the knee, but not so badly as to prevent him from standing. "Moore advanced toward him," says Ramsey, who got the story from Moore, "and the Indian threw his tomahawk, but missed him. Moore sprang at him with his large butcher knife drawn, which the Indian caught by the blade, and attempted to wrest from the hand of his antagonist. Holding on with desperate tenacity to the knife, both clinched with their left hands. A scuffle ensued in which the Indian was thrown to the ground, his right hand being nearly severed and bleeding profusely. Moore, still holding the handle of the knife in the right hand, succeeded with the other to disengage his own tomahawk from his belt, and ended the strife by sinking it into the skull of the Indian."

But what of affairs at the Watauga fort?

Agreeably to plans which had been divulged to the whites, the attack of a body under Chief Old Abraham was made on that station the same day. He was to attack Fort Lee, in the Nollichucky settlement, but the inhabitants had dismantled its fortifications and retreated to Watauga.

The defense at the latter place numbered only forty, under the command of James Robertson, who was afterwards to figure conspicuously in the Middle Tennessee section.

The Indians attacked at sunrise, but were repulsed with loss. They skulked around the fort for three weeks, finally retreating on the appoach of assistance from Virginia. During the siege they captured Mrs. William Bean, and killed some men and boys who were making their way to the fort for protection. A boy by the name of Moore was carried to one of their towns and burned at the stake. "The garrison was only forty men strong," observes Phelan, "but they were under the command of an officer not less resolute, not less fertile in resources, not less cool in the presence of danger, than the Englishman who, three years later, gained immortality and an English peerage by the defense of Gibraltar against equally overwhelming odds. The achievements of one were viewed with wondering admiration by the civilization of the world. The achievements of the other, though not less worthy of all honor and renown, were performed under the shadows of a primitive forest in a frontier fort, against unrecorded savages. James Robertson deserves for his memorable defense of the Watauga fort a place not less illustrious in the annals of Tennessee than that accorded to Lord Heathfield in the annals of England. More than three hundred Indians were held at bay by less than forty men capable of service, and despite stratagems, and all the arts and cunning of an Indian warfare, midnight attacks and daily onslaughts, were eventually compelled to raise the siege and retire."

A third body of Indians, commanded by The Raven, went up Carter's Valley, but finding the people shut up in forts, returned to their towns. Another band which came up the Clinch, visited with fire and tomahawk the whole country from what is now Sullivan County to Seven-Mile Ford, in Virginia. But North Carolina and Virginia sent bodies of troops to protect the frontiers, and these, with the settlers, entered the Cherokee country, compelling the Indians to sue for peace and to cede much of their territory.

CHAPTER IV.

JOHN SEVIER, SOLDIER AND STATESMAN, AS WELL AS
A NOTICE OF THE STATE OF FRANKLIN.

Few States of the Union have had as citizens a greater number of men of pronounced individuality than Tennessee—men who, if they had lived in other epochs, might have had their deeds ineradicably impressed on the preserving tablets of the centuries. Place and occasion have much to do in making living names. No matter how much originality and genius one has, these attributes may not be recognized unless circumstances intervene in their behalf. Admiral Dewey, whose brilliant genius conceived the masterful stroke at Manila in the war between America and Spain, would have perhaps died without being considered above mediocrity as a naval officer had the war never materialized. If our civil war had not occurred, would Grant and Lee, Sherman and Jackson, Meade and Johnston have had the reputation which is theirs?

Had Gustavus A. Henry, of Tennessee, been given the part in Roman history filled by Cicero, he would have acted it so perfectly that the world would not have missed the chief of Roman orators. Henry Watterson would have wielded as trenchant and scholarly a pen in the domain of criticism as Jeffrey. Robert L. Taylor, who might have been a great actor or poet if he had not been an orator, and in whose composition are strangely blended the highest type of humor and pathos, statecraft and the plain wisdom of the every-day man, power to sway by eloquence and deprive hatred of its venom by the subtlety of his badinage—would be one of the most versatile and brilliant figures of the times had he been born in an era and a sphere where originality is given the opportunity which it must generally await.

Although but lately becoming appreciated by the public at large for his excellencies, perhaps no Tennessean since the first settler's cabin was built in the State has stood so high for such length of time in the affections of the people of the commonwealth he assisted so materially in building as Gen. John Sevier.

He was identified with the first days of the Watauga Association; was early made colonel of Washington County; assisted in running down Ferguson, the gallant British general, and in bringing about the capture of his command at King's Mountain—which battle was the turning point of the war between the colonies and England; took part with Gen. Francis Marion in the closing scenes of the revolution; and from the close of the war till the cession to the United States by North Carolina, in 1784, of all the territory which is now the State of Tennessee, he spent the greater part of his time protecting the frontiers and chastising the Indians for their depredations upon the whites. It can be very readily surmised that with such a career the popularity of Sevier among his countrymen must have been considerable, and their confidence in him great; and that should a crisis arise in their affairs he would be the person to whom they would look for guidance.

That crisis was coming.

The Assembly of North Carolina, during the April session in 1784, appreciating the burdens under which Congress was then laboring—the harassment of public debt and the clamor of creditors—resolved to act upon the suggestion that "States owning vacant lands throw them into the common stock for defraying the expenses of the late war." It ceded all the territory which constitutes Tennessee, if Congress would accept it within two years. When the settlers heard of this —believing that they would be left without any form of government for two years, during which time they could not hope for protection or assistance from either North Carolina or the United States—they were naturally enraged. They reasoned that the East Tennessee settlements—where really the only disaffection existed—were not entitled to a superior court, and so crime would have to go unpunished; it was not lawful for a brigadier-general to call into service the militia of the county, and therefore what protection could they have from the Indians, who were still aggressive and intent on checking the growth of the settlements?

TALK OF SEPARATION.

In moments of resentment and distrust, a falsehood, having a modicum of speciousness, may for a while really get the ascendency of truth; and there were not wanting ambitious spirits to mislead and frighten the people with probabilities that were very remote, to say the least. There were, too, many persons who were honest enough in the belief that the settlers had not only been mistreated, but that unless a separate government were formed by the Western settlements, their very existence would be jeopardized; Sevier was among the latter class.

The people became more excited as the weeks went by, and though later on the Assembly repealed the cession act and acceded to other demands of the settlers, forming the militia into a brigade and making Sevier brigadier-general among other things, they clamored still for separation. Sevier himself on the 14th of December, 1784, after the Assembly had met and adjourned, addressed the electors assembled at Jonesborough, saying that "the grievances which the people complained of are redressed, and my recommendation to them is that they proceed no further in their design to separate from North Carolina." He more than once urged this view, but unfortunately Capt. William Cocke in an interview with him erased the impression he had received toward the government of North Carolina. The movement to separate was carried out, and as might have been expected, since he was the most popular person in the discontented settlements, John Sevier was in 1785 elected Governor by the assembly of the new State, which was given the name of Franklin, with its capital at Greeneville.

As Gilmore correctly contends, Sevier made a great mistake in allowing himself to be forced into the leadership of the new State, which was destined to be of such short duration. It was perhaps the mistake of his life, and not only brought him enemies and made him an outlaw for awhile, but really came very nearly involving him in a trouble with Spain, which would have turned the course of his destiny from that honorable groove which ultimately led to fame and a grateful people's love.

The new State—the predecessor of Tennessee—was short-lived. One of the chief causes for its toppling was the growing sentiment among the Franklin people themselves for reconciliation with North Carolina. John Tipton, who at the beginning of the talk of separation was an ardent friend of the cause, was one of the most prominent deserters. This, it has been said, was through his jealousy of Sevier because the latter was looked to in reverence by the people and honored with the highest office in their gift. The fact that one fails to be thus selected is not always indicative of a lack of fitness; witness the failure of Clay and Webster. But in the case of Tipton it was different. He was courageous, but not possessed of great intellectual force. He became Sevier's bitterest critic, as well as an implacable enemy to the cause

A MERCILESS ENEMY.

dear to Sevier's heart, the success of the new State. The person who has been an abettor in an undertaking, and then changes and reforms because of a change of circumstances or because he sees more clearly, is apt to be considered vacillating. If he becomes a boisterous and malignant changeling, he is then almost certainly regarded as a renegade. The public has formed the latter estimate of Tipton, and it will be a task for the historian to change this idea.

After Sevier became governor of Franklin, Tipton inaugurated a relentless war on him until the new State collapsed in 1788. Though Sevier was necessarily chagrined by his failure, this enemy was still too vindictive to show generosity. He it was who arrested the ex-governor and had him placed in irons. While a number of their acquaintances and comrades were at Jonesborough in November, 1788, says Haywood, giving a succinct description of the interesting border episode, Sevier came riding into town with ten or twelve men. This was soon after his return from an expedition against the Cherokees. "There he drank freely," continues the historian, "and in a short time a controversy arose between him and Major Craig, who at that time lived where Maryville now stands, respecting the killing of those friendly Indians in the spring of the year, which occasioned the war with them that then existed.* Craig censured Sevier

---
*This has reference to the Kirk butchery, mentioned in Chapter X of this work.

for not preventing the murder, Craig having been present when it happened, and under the command of Sevier. Those who were present interposed, and brought them to friendly terms. The general (Martin, who was of the number), Maj. King, and Col. Love left them and set off for Col. Love's house, fourteen miles distant. Not being able to go that far, Gen. Martin and King stopped at a house near Col. Robinson's. After they left Jonesborough another quarrel arose between Sevier and Caldwell, the former advancing with a pistol in his hand, and Caldwell with a rock. The pistol accidentally fired, and shot one of Sevier's men in the abdomen. Shortly after this Sevier left Jonesborough and came by a place near Col. Robinson's, where Col. Love had taken up and stopped at Robinson's still house, where they all drank freely, and after some time separated. After Sevier left Jonesborough, Caldwell, with whom he had quarreled, went to Tipton, and in going and returning collected eight or ten men, with whom he went in pursuit of Sevier. Arriving at the house where Col. Love lodged, he went with them to Col. Robinson's where Gen. Martin and Maj. King were. Tipton there had a close search made for Sevier, supposing that as there was a good understanding between Robinson and him, the latter might be there. The pursuers then went to the widow Brown's, where Sevier was. Tipton and the party with him rushed forward to the door of common entrance. It was about sunrise.

Mrs. Brown had just risen. Seeing a party with arms at that early hour, well acquainted with Col. Tipton, probably rightly apprehending the cause of this visit, she sat herself down in the front door to prevent their getting into the house, which caused a considerable bustle between her and Col. Tipton. Sevier had slept near one end of the house, and on hearing the noise sprung from his bed, and, looking through a hole in the door-side, saw Col. Love, upon which he opened the door and held out his hand, saying to Col. Love:

"'I surrender to you.'

"He was in his undress, and Col. Love led him to the place where Tipton and Mrs. Brown were contending about a passage into the house. Tipton, on seeing Sevier, was greatly enraged, and swore that he would hang him. Tipton held a pistol in his hand, sometimes swearing that he would shoot him, and Sevier really was afraid that he would put his threat into execution. Tipton at last became calm, and ordered Sevier to get his horse, for that he would carry him to Jonesborough."

Haywood has given the outlines of a typical border scene, and those who have witnessed similar occurrences in some back-country neighborhood can resort to the memory to give the affair the proper coloring. The dirt road leading through a mountainous and, at that season, bleak country; the scattered log cabins from which at the approach of the crowd women and children emerged to get a glimpse of Nollichucky Jack, who in the gallant way he had saluted them graciously; the little streams running across the road, where the horses paused to slake their thirst; perhaps some loud talking now and then, wherein gasconade entered largely—for the border product, the bully, was not lacking in most collections. The proceedings at the still house form a striking feature of the picture, as do the pursuit by Caldwell and Tipton, and the latter's swagger and bluster as he thought he at last had his hated rival where he could crush him.

When the prisoner arrived at Jonesborough, Tipton ordered him put in irons, and from there had him taken to Morganton, where he had no doubt "outraged law" would make an example of the ex-governor.

But Sevier had friends who did not forsake him. As hate had been the prime factor in this offense against his liberties, it is somewhat natural for Tennesseans, at least, to feel a thrill of pleasure over the outcome of the arrest; for persecution usually arouses sympathy for the victim in the bosoms of those who like fair play.

A few days afterwards, Sevier's trial was being held at Morganton, North Carolina. The crowd in attendance was of course large, owing to the wide reputation of the Indian fighter and audacious leader of the young commonwealth which had caused the State so much trouble. Sevier might or might not have been uneasy regarding the result of the investigation. He had not seen his old friends, James Cozby and

THE RESCUE. 41

Nathaniel Evans, when they rode up in front of the court-house, and left standing there a splendid thoroughbred horse which was owned by Sevier; but when the two entered the court room, he sized up the situation quickly, and prepared to act.

Cozby, narrates Phelan, stepped in front of the judge, and in a loud voice asked if he was done with that man, pointing to Sevier. In the midst of the confusion produced by this unexpected interlude, Sevier made a rush for the door, sprang upon his horse, and was soon far up the mountain road, where he was joined by a party of friends.* There was no further effort to try him. He was even elected to the North Carolina senate from Greene County, and was allowed to take his seat. Not only this, he was soon appointed brigadier-general of the western counties; and Tipton finally saw that it was useless to try to repress him and wisely gave up, though his hatred lasted through life.

Sevier's popularity was swift and permanent. Soon after his reconciliation with North Carolina he was elected to Congress. He was for six terms governor of Tennessee, and elected to Congress again in 1811. In 1815 he was appointed by President Monroe to locate the boundary lines of the Creek territory, and died in Alabama on September 24, 1815. His remains

---

*This dramatic incident—the rescue of Sevier—is declared by later writers than Phelan to be a fiction. But all proceedings against him were suddenly stopped.

were removed from Alabama in 1889, and re-interred in the court-house yard at Knoxville, where a suitable granite monument now marks the last resting-place of the dust of one of whom it can be truthfully said,

> "Whatever record leap to light,
> He never shall be shamed."

For some unaccountable reason, Sevier's memory has been allowed to fall into neglect. He was honest, chivalrous, devoted to his family, indefatigable in his efforts to protect and further the interests of the pioneers, a gallant officer in the revolutionary war, an able statesman and without guile, and, as before remarked, no public man of Tennessee has approached him in personal popularity, if we except, perhaps, Hon. Robert L. Taylor. The tributes of the historians are worth much. They are unstinted in Sevier's case. Says Haywood, who died only about a decade after Sevier passed away: "He was among the frontier people, who adored him. He had by nature a talent for acquiring popular favor. He had a friendly demeanor, a pleasing address, and, to crown all, he was a soldier." Gilmore, in a historical work published in 1898, observes: "I have called him a hero, a soldier, and a statesman; but he was more than all of these; he was a civilizer, a good organizer, a nation-builder." And Phelan pays him this deserved tribute: "To say that he was in his sphere a statesman of the first order of ability, and that as a warrior he was excelled by none

A Great Figure.

who engaged in the same mode of warfare, and that he never lost a battle, claims for him a high place among the great men of the world. Only he acted on a small stage. There can be no doubt that he is the greatest figure in Tennessee history, and there is as little doubt that outside the mountains and valleys of East Tennessee he is, from a popular standpoint, as little known as if he had been one of the shepherd kings of Egypt."

It is hoped that before the fad of "revivals" shall have come to an end, the public will awaken fully to the worth of this interesting American.

CHAPTER V.

THE SETTLING OF MIDDLE TENNESSEE, NOTING THE BEGINNING OF INDIAN ATROCITIES.

In one of the histories of Tennessee it is held that the first settler of Middle Tennessee was a trapper by the name of Thomas Sharpe Spencer. He arrived on the Cumberland in 1778 with a few companions, but considering the dangers surrounding the forming of a settlement too great, all but Spencer returned. He took up his abode in a large hollow tree near what is now known as Castalian Springs, in Sumner County, and remained there through the winter. "He saw no one and heard not the sound of a human voice," to quote Phelan. "It is related as historically true that he passed once not far from the cabin in which dwelt a hunter in the service of De Mumbreun, and that the hunter, seeing the imprint of his enormous foot, became frightened and fled through the wilderness to the French settlements on the Wabash. His gigantic figure, alone in the midst of the endless forests, wandering and hunting throughout their vast depths, the herald of a coming civilization, cool, courageous, and self-reliant, going to sleep at night by a solitary camp-fire, with the hooting of the owls and the screaming of panthers around him and with no assurance of the absence of a deadlier foe, is one of the most picturesque in the history of southwestern pioneers." But in 1769-70 Casper Mansker, Abraham Bledsoe and John Rains visited as hunters and explorers the east side of Cumberland river; and in the year 1771, Mansker, accompanied by Joseph Drake, Isaac Bledsoe and others, visited the country. Again, in 1775, Mansker arrived in the Cumberland region, but no one remained, so that Spencer seemed really the earliest to have a well-defined mission as a pioneer.

Within a year from Spencer's arrival quite a number of emigrants reached the Cumberland and built cabins and cast their corn crops. Among these were James Robertson, properly called the founder of Middle Tennessee, George Freeland, William Neelly, Edward Swanson, James Hanly, Mark Robertson, Zachariah Wells and William Overall, and a negro man. After their arrival another small party under Casper Mansker joined them. They settled near the Sulphur Spring on the site of Nashville, not far from the ruins of the cabin built some years before by the French trader, De Munbreun. Later on Robertson's company was to be joined by their families as well as additional settlers under the guidance of Col. John Donelson, who were to make their journey by water. There were some women and children with the Mansker party.

When the settlers came to the Salt Lick, the present

site of Nashville, there was no evidence that the country had ever been in cultivation. "Nothing was presented to the eye," says Haywood, "but one large plain of woods and cane, frequented by buffalos, elk, deer, wolves, foxes, panthers and other animals suited to the climate. The land adjacent to the French Lick which Mr. Mansker in 1769 called an old field, was a large open piece, frequented and trodden by buffalo, whose large paths led to it from all parts of the country, and there concentred. On these adjacent lands was no undergrowth nor cane as far as the creek reached in time of high water; or, rather, as far as the backwater reached. The country as far as to Elk river and beyond it, had not a single permanent inhabitant except the wild beasts of the forest, but it had been inhabited many centuries before by a numerous population. At every lasting spring is a large collection of graves, made in a particular way, with the heads inclined on the sides and feet stones, the whole covered with a stratum of mold and dirt about eight or ten inches deep. At many springs is the appearance of walls inclosing ancient habitations, the foundations of which were visible wherever the earth was cleared and cultivated, to which walls entrenchments were sometimes added. These walls sometimes inclose six, eight or ten acres of land; and often they are more extensive. Judging from the number and frequency of these appearances, it cannot be estimated but that the former inhabitants were ten times, if not twenty times, more numerous than those who at present (1823) occupy the country."

The winter of 1779-80 was an unusually severe one, and the pioneers experienced a rough time. There was nothing for their stock to subsist upon but cut cane. The settlers sustained life by eating bear and buffalo meat; while in February heavy and continuous rains set in.

They saw nothing of the Indians until January, 1780. Early in that month some of the settlers who had been in the woods in pursuit of game discovered tracks, which they surmised were Indians' from the fact that moccasins were worn, and the toes of the tracks were none of them turned outward like those of white people. Their suspicions proved correct. A party of about sixty Delaware Indians made the footprints. They came from the direction of Caney Fork river, and camped near the head of Mill Creek. When questioned by the whites, they claimed that they had only come into the neighborhood to hunt. It is believed that they were the first Indians to molest the whites on the Cumberland.

Robertson's party soon saw the necessity of taking shelter in blockhouses and stations. That at the bluffs, Nashborough, was the principal station, but others were built—Freeland's, north of Nashborough; Eaton's, on the east bank of the river; Gasper's, ten miles north at the present town of Goodlettsville; Asher's, three miles from Gallatin; Bledsoe's, eight miles from Gallatin; Donelson's, on Stone's river, near the Stone's River bridge on the Lebanon and Nashville pike; and Fort Union, in a bend of the river six miles above Nashborough. Laws similar to those for the government of the Watauga Association were also made.

The caution of the settlers was timely, for they were not long to remain undisturbed.

In April, 1780, the Indians began a series of butcheries which lasted in the Cumberland settlement for years. In that month Keywood and Milliken, two hunters, coming to the fort, stopped on Richland Creek, five or six miles west of Nashborough, and as Keywood stepped down to the bank of the creek to drink the Indians fired upon Milliken and killed him. Murders were after this committed almost every day for months by the Indians, who regarded neither age nor sex. In many instances they cut off the victims' heads. Mansker's station was broken up, the stationers fleeing to Nashborough and to Kentucky; and the Renfroes and their relatives who founded a settlement on Red river at the present site of the little city of Clarksville were driven away, and on their return for their property were massacred. Donelson's Station was also abandoned. It is hardly a matter for wonder that a number of the settlers returned to the older colonies, while others would have gone had it not been for the scarcity of horses.

James Robertson discouraged retreat. Few men have shown a more stubborn resistance to failure, a bolder front to disaster. "There are characters whom we admire with even and impassionate serenity but upon whom we rely with utter abandon," says a biographer. "Robertson's character was of this kind. It was wellbuilt, with solid masonry and broad foundations. He is eminently trustworthy. We are filled with a kind of joyous admiration of our humanity when we see blended in him so much modesty and so much fortitude. He possessed rather fortitude than bravery. The lack of fear was such a part of his being that we learn to take it as a matter of course. It was a part of the times and the people. But his fortitude lifts him to an altitude. It never wavers, it never quails, it never retreats."

He had early taken his position as leader, and he performed prodigies to encourage the settlers and to insure their safety and success.

CHAPTER VI.

FURTHER MENTION OF EVENTS IN THE CUMBERLAND SETTLEMENTS AND JAMES ROBERTSON'S ACHIEVEMENTS.

John Sevier was the most prominent frontiersman of the East Tennessee settlements, but James Robertson won enviable distinction at Watauga and in the Cumberland community as a pioneer. He was a native of Virginia, having been born in Brunswick County on June 28, 1742. He visited the Watauga and Boone's Creek settlement in East Tennessee in 1770. After having made a crop there through assistance rendered by a settler named Honeycut, he returned to North Carolina. The next year, however, he again joined the Watauga colony and took an active interest in the formation of the Watauga association and in its subsequent affairs. This association was probably formed in 1772, as stated, and was the first scheme of government ever devised for the people occupying Tennessee soil.

As early as 1772 Robertson was found by his fellow-settlers to possess a judgment which they could rely upon. In that year a line was run between Virginia and the Cherokee hunting grounds, and it left the Wataugans within the boundaries of the latter, whereupon it was decided to make an effort to secure a lease from the Indians. It was secured by Robertson and John Boon. After this was accomplished the event was celebrated by gymnastics and races by the whites and Indians; but in the evening of the day of the celebration one of the Indians was slain by some men from Wolf's Hill, Virginia, who were taking part in the exercises. The murder was impolitic as well as wanton, and would have produced dire retaliatory results had it not been for Robertson, who made a journey to the chief town of the Indians, a hundred and fifty miles away, to appease them by a promise to punish the murderer or murderers if to be found. The courage evinced in this instance and on subsequent occasions was probably remembered when the attack was a few years afterwards made on Watauga Fort by Old Abraham, and insured his command of that post. His heroic defense thereof is mentioned in a previous chapter.

Some time in 1778 he decided to emigrate to a point on the Cumberland river, and with a party of eight set out through Cumberland Gap, finally reaching the section where Nashville stands. In this new enterprise he acted in conjunction with John Donelson, of Virginia, afterwards the father-in-law of Andrew Jackson.

From his arrival at the Great Salt Lick in 1779, Robertson naturally took the leadership, devising a form of government for the settlers in conjunction with Col. Richard Henderson (who really instigated the Cumberland settlement), encouraging them through all their difficulties, fighting and planning and using diplomacy as occasion required, and justly earning his title of father of Middle Tennessee.

Reference is made elsewhere to the difficulties besetting the settlers during their first months on the Cumberland. Though quite a number of emigrants had arrived, and Nashborough, Union, Gasper's, Bledsoe's, Asher's, Freeland's and Eaton's forts had been erected, the whites were decimated by marauding Indians; hearts were burdened by news of the massacre of the Renfroe settlement, established near the site of Clarksville by Moses Renfroe in the year 1779; game was driven out of the immediate neighborhood; food had become so scarce that walnuts and hickorynuts had to be saved by the cart load as winter edibles, while the supply of powder was running short. The idea of leaving their homes began to find lodgment in the minds of the settlers. During the crisis Robertson agreed if they would remain on the Cumberland, to go where ammunition could be had and obtain a supply, and this he did—ran the gauntlet, as one historian pertinently observes.

On his return from his perilous journey on January 15, 1781, he stopped for the night at Fort Freeland, and was thereby instrumental in saving its inmates from massacre. That night the settlers had been careless enough to retire without appointing a guard. The

A NIGHT ATTACK. 53

night was cold and clear, and the winter moon threw a mantle over the sleeping lowlands and around the rugged shoulders of the surrounding hills. The quietude of a dream-scene hovered over the blockhouses; the rough palisades running from house to house were transformed into a strange beauty, frost-covered and scintillating. Like shifting silhouettes, a band of Indians approached, blending with the shadows of the pickets and cabins. A half a hundred gathered, and crept closer to the gate, which was secured with a chain. One of the boldest reached the clasp, but in loosening it caused such a noise, despite his carefulness, as to awaken Robertson. Springing from his bed, the pioneer gave the cry of "Indians!" It was none too soon, for as he gave the warning the savages were crowding through the gate. The settlers seized their guns and began firing into the ranks of the intruders, who retreated, firing as they ran, when the entrance was again secured. A negro belonging to Robertson was killed, but no other harm was sustained.

The distress of the settlers continued, despite the efforts of the more energetic and courageous to ameliorate their troubles. The Indians had adopted the policy of driving the game from the country, prosecuting it vigorously through the fall of 1780 and the winter of 1781. The stationers were therefore forced to go to distant sections to procure food, encountering many dangers. On one occasion a party of twenty men went up Caney Fork as high as Flynn's creek, and after being out only a few days returned with one hundred and five bears, seventy-five buffalos and eighty odd deer.

As James Robertson had been proving his worthiness to lead, his wife soon showed that she was a helpmeet indeed, and a heroine. It is said by Putnam and Gilmore that it was her forethought and courage that figured materially in the settlers' victory in the "Battle of the Bluffs," which assured, in 1781, the continuance of the settlements. That battle, though few were involved on either side, was one of the really thrilling events of southwestern border warfare.

The fort at Nashborough was erected upon the bluff between the southeast corner of the square and Spring street (so as to include a bold spring which then issued from that point). It was a log building two stories high, with portholes and lookout stations. Other log houses were near it, and all enclosed with palisades or pickets firmly set in the earth, having the upper ends sharpened. There was one large entrance, with the lookout station above for the guard. From this point the country could be viewed for miles in two directions, but the view was obstructed to the west and southwest by a thick forest of cedar trees, beneath which there was a dense growth of privet bushes. Upon lands with deeper soil and less rock, instead of cedar and privet, there were forest trees of large growth, and thick canebrakes. The country was well suited to a skulking enemy and for ambushing purposes.

BATTLE OF THE BLUFFS.

On the night of April 1, 1781, or early in the morning of April 2, a large body of Cherokees ventured near the fort of Nashborough and formed an ambush. After daylight three bucks fired at the fort and ran off. Nineteen of the settlers mounted their horses and, rushing out, pursued them. Gilmore says that Robertson was among the number of pursuers. The historians are generally silent on this point. If he was of the number his usual caution seemed to have deserted him on that occasion.

When the whites had gone a considerable distance from the fort, reaching a branch, they discovered Indians in the creek and in the nearby underbrush. The latter arose and fired a volley at the horsemen, who dismounted to give them battle. A number of the whites were killed—Peter Gill, Alexander Buchanan, George Kennedy, Zachariah White and Capt. Leiper; and James Manifee, Joseph Moonshaw and Isaac Lucas were wounded.

Presently another body of savages were discovered. They were hid in the brush and cedars, and were evidently intending to rush into the fort in the rear of the combatants. But the horses of the settlers broke loose when the firing was going on, and a number of the Indians went in pursuit of them, while the whites, seeing that they were being cut off, attempted to regain the fort. Would they succeed? The chances were certainly for a period against them. Their horses were gone; the Indians were swarming around them in overwhelming numbers; taken by surprise, the settlers were badly demoralized.

Meanwhile those who were left at the fort were naturally in a state of the greatest anxiety. They could not see those who had gone out to battle, but their riderless horses, dashing by the fort, led them to believe the nineteen had been killed or captured. The fort, they thought, would next be attacked, and they resolved to sell their lives dearly. Even the women took guns and axes to assist in repelling the expected assault.

Mrs. Robertson happened to think of the dogs in the fort, which were yelping and endeavoring to get out. The animals had been trained to hate the Indians. Abe Castleman, one of the first settlers, had a dog named Red Gill, which would leave the trail of a bear or other wild animal to follow that of an Indian. Why not turn the raving pack outside in this hour of extremity? Acting on the impulse, Mrs. Robertson ordered the gate opened. The dogs rushed through the open, over the eminences, and made such a fierce attack on the Indians, whose line had not yet been broken, that they were compelled to defend themselves from the canine foe instead of endeavoring to capture or kill the whites. Then those left alive of the latter, noting the diversion, and taking advantage of it, made for the fort, all but two reaching it in safety. These two were Isaac Lucas and Edward Swanson. The former had his thigh broken by a ball, and was left by his

Result of the Battle.

comrades. The Indians wanted his scalp, and some of them ran toward him. He killed the one nearest, and continued dragging himself toward the station. Other savages attempted to reach him, but the stationers kept up such a brisk fire upon them that the brave fellow finally reached the gate and was taken in.

Swanson, in retreating toward the fort, was pursued by an Indian, who placed his gun against him, attempting to fire; the gun only snapped. Swanson grasped the weapon, twisting it to one side and spilling the priming from the pan. The Indian then struck him with the gun barrel; he then delivered a second blow, this time with the stock. This knocked Swanson down on all fours. John Buchanan, seeing Swanson's situation, ran to his relief, shooting at the Indian. The latter retired to a stump, and Swanson and Buchanan made their escape.

This battle practically decided the fate of the Cumberland settlements. The assailants were completely discomfited.

That night another party of Indians came near the fort and fired upon it, but a swivel, loaded with gravel and pieces of pots, was discharged at them and they withdrew.

James Robertson had been made colonel, which gave him command of the military equipment of the various stations. In 1783 he was elected a member of the General Assembly of North Carolina, and it was after his return to Nashborough from his duties as representative at Tarborough, that he found the conditions about as desperate as they had been for many months; children were killed and "chopped" by small prowling bands of savages; men were shot from ambush and their bodies split. In May, 1787, Mark, a brother of Col. Robertson, was killed. These outrages were traced to Indians living near the Muscle Shoals, in the Tennessee river, and Robertson resolved at last to invade their retreats. Two friendly Chickasaws, one of them known as Toka, offered to become guides, and were accepted.

A force of one hundred and twenty men was gathered and placed under Col. Robertson's command. In addition to this, some boats containing provisions were sent around, these being commanded by David Hay.

The march was made as rapidly as possible, and late one evening the force stopped within hearing of the rapids. Campfires were made, supper was prepared and eaten, and the band of avengers, with their intrepid leader, spread their buffalo robes and blankets on the ground, and in groups conversed of the topic uppermost in their minds—the Indians and their depredations. The roar of the distant falls was mellowed into tones low and soft as the bass notes of some vast musical instrument played by unseen fingers; wild animals, attracted by the aroma from the camp, prowled among the underbrush at a safe distance from the light; the fragrance of wild flowers, bruised by some passing hoof, came in upon the breeze ever and anon;

and above all, the stars twinkled like the campfires of nomads in the upper desert.

The night passed without an attack from the Indians. Were they unaware of the approach of the whites? At dawn the troops were mounted and soon on the march; and by noon had reached the river. While spies were sent out to search for the path which the Indian guides said led to a crossing, the main body sought concealment until night.

The Indian town they intended attacking lay near a large spring, where the town of Tuscumbia, Ala., now stands. It was on the farther side of the stream, the Creeks and Cherokees occupying that side of the Tennessee. The inhabitants of the village were mostly Creeks, and a more desperate set could not have been found among all the tribes.

The spies, in their reconnoitering, discovered some savages on the opposite bank, apparently on the lookout for the invading party; for they passed about cautiously from tree to tree in a stooping posture. After awhile they entered a canoe, and paddled it into the river some distance; then, evidently suspecting no foes near, they plunged into the water for a bath and swim, finally returning to the bank and disappearing in the cane. Capt. Rains, with a squad of fifteen men, had been ordered up the river to look for Indians and a crossing place, but making no discoveries, he returned about sunset to the main body.

Col. Robertson resolved to attempt a crossing at daylight the next morning at the point where the Indians had been seen bathing, some of the scouts proposing to swim over and bring back the canoe which had been used by the savages. These scouts, while on the mission for the canoe, had also gone out and examined some nearby cabins and found them deserted.

After patching up the boat the troops finally succeeded in crossing, some therein, others clinging to the sides, while a number swam upon or beside their horses. "With the exception of those who had passed over in the boat," Putnam declares, "most of them were there with their clothes perfectly wet. Some had put their clothes in their hats or tied them around their heads and hats, hoping thus to keep them dry. But during the time allowed for their horses to eat some corn, and for the men to breakfast off jerked venison and parched corn, the wet clothes were hung upon the bushes to dry. An army in dishabille! An invading army within six miles of the enemy's stronghold, and on the enemy's side of that broad river! They themselves described their whole appearance as most laughable."

As they prepared to move a considerable shower came up, making the journey through the woods somewhat disagreeable. The path through the barrens, Toka, the guide, said, led to the cornfields near the Indian town. Reaching the fields, and then Cold Water Creek, they perceived the town on the opposite side. The Chickasaws suggested that upon discovering them the Indians would flee to their boats at the mouth of the creek, and Capt. Rains was ordered with a few men to intercept the enemy in case this prediction should prove true. The main body then struck a double-quick, crossed the creek and were soon in the town. Many of the inhabitants fled precipitately to their boats, and were in the act of shoving off into the river when the men under Capt. Rains fell upon them, and the work of slaughter began—those under Robertson engaging as soon as they reached the scene. Twenty-six Indians were killed in the boats and the river. Three French traders and a white woman were also killed and one or two Indian women captured. There were few women seen; and it is surmised that Indians like those—thieves and murderers, who had collected there—probably had no wives and children with them.

The town was burned, and the whites camped that night near the ruins. Next morning they began their homeward march, reaching the settlements after an absence of nineteen days, and without the loss of a man.

The party which started by water under Hay was less successful. Reaching the mouth of Duck river, one of the boats was fired into by Indians concealed on the bank, at which fire Joseph Renfroe was killed and John Top, Hugh Rogan and Edward Hogan were wounded. After a consultation the party concluded to return home.

When the settlements were made into a territory,

and William Blount appointed Governor, Robertson became brigadier-general of the Mero District, the name now given to the Cumberland settlements. In 1791, at the time of the Holston Treaty, he visited the Cherokee nation, seeking to dissuade them from further hostilities, but their aggressions were but temporarily stayed. In 1792 the Creeks hoped to throw the Cumberland people off their guard, and a number of their chiefs visited Gen. Robertson at Nashville to smoke the pipe of peace. While he received them cordially, he was not deceived; and continued to strengthen the militia. The inroads of the savages were not discontinued, which testified to the foresight and judgment of Gen. Robertson, although Gov. Blount was often led to believe in the Indians' protests of friendship. These aggressions drove the people into a determination to retaliate. As much as he regarded the orders of Gov. Blount to prevent an incursion into the enemy's country, patience at last ceased to be a virtue; and on September 6, 1794, he ordered the destruction of some of the Cherokee towns. The point of attack was the five lower towns of the Chickamaugas—a tribe of the Cherokees, notorious above all the Indians for treachery, hatred of the whites and courage—of which the village of Nickojack had the greatest notoriety. The incursion, known as the Nickojack Expedition, the outcome of which brought comparative peace to the settlers of Tennessee, will be treated in another chapter.

ENTERTAINING INDIANS. 63

Robertson was reprimanded severely and unjustly for this chastisement of the Indians, and was so much wounded thereby that he tendered his resignation, but nothing more came of the matter.

After Gen. Robertson had ceased to act as brigadier-general of Mero District, he retained his office of Temporary Agent to the Chickasaws and Choctaws; and during this time was often annoyed by visiting Indians who, though friendly, proved their capacity to bore. A notice of one of these visits may not be uninteresting in this sketch. In January, 1795, he was informed by Colbert and other Chickasaw chiefs that they, with several warriors and a number of women and children, would visit him at Nashville.

They arrived promptly, and an effort was made to make them enjoy themselves. The entertainment of a hundred hungry Indians was necessarily expensive, and a few persons contributed corn, meal and meat, while some of the chiefs and their families were lodged in the houses of the citizens. On one occasion a grand dinner party was gotten up by subscription to do honor to "General" Colbert; it was quite an affair for that day. Rev. Thomas B. Craighead was a Presbyterian minister who had been among the settlers for years, undergoing all the vicissitudes of frontier life for the sake of his Maker; and at one of his services during their sojourn Colbert and his staff were attendants.

The entertainment accorded savage guests by Gen. Robertson is described by Putnam: "We have never heard of such marked and flattering attentions paid to these more than half-naked savages, as were sometimes given by Gen. Robertson, to tame their savage natures and secure their good will," he narrates: "They uniformly called him 'a good man;' and such a scene as was exhibited at the last Chickasaw visit to the General might well employ the skill of a Hogarth. Beneath the lofty and beautiful maples which surrounded Gen. Robertson's station, might be seen a variety of the copper-colored race, mostly crouched upon the ground. The best dressed of the females have a sack (not overly long, yet long enough to hide the strip of 'stroud' or baize around the waist and hips), with moccasins and leggings, ornamented by beads and tinkling bells; and across the shoulders a dirty blanket. The hair is braided and hangs down like a mandarin's. Such was the attire of Jacsic Moniac, the wife of 'General' Colbert. She had around her a full representation of the half-breed general—the parents' 'small arms.' Near by sat Molle-tulla, the tall wife of the mountain leader, 'Captain' Piomingo, whom General Robertson had instructions to equip with clothing and ornaments. There were others, the better-halves of chiefs and warriors of great pretensions and little worth. If we could transfer another group of Creeks, and stand or seat them not afar off, and such as Gen. Robertson not long before entertained, we should see the partner of the Mad-dog and her whelps, the Turkey and her brood, the Hanging Maw, and all that set of gourmands. And now, with all this crew, unwashed, uncombed, unclouted—and unhung, seated or moving around that tall and sedate person, mark how he pats their heads and smiles at their recognition. Who else but Gen. Robertson would pause in such a group, and, dipping his finger in the vermilion which the squaw held in one hand, and the black paint in the box, would give to the faces of these not naturally ill-looking urchins the wrinkled appearance of a monkey, the head of a cat, of the wily fox or sly raccoon!"

This treatment of the Indians by Gen. Robertson gives us a key to his character, and may go far toward explaining the alleged "intrigues" with Spain, afterwards charged against him. It is true that the diplomat's strength and success may lie as much in that suavity which permits the other party to draw flattering conclusions from the diplomat's actions if he wishes, as in his dignity and unyielding attitude. While having no admiration for the Indians, Gen. Robertson had too much judgment to let them believe he was not all appreciation. Bent on placating the Spanish authorities in America for the sake of the struggling settlement looking to him for guidance, he did not feel himself at fault if Gov. Mero, the Spanish representative, misconstrued his friendship. He trusted that his well-known Americanism, as well as his reputation for probity, would shield him from the suspicion of desiring to forsake his country for Spain— of wishing to become a subject of Spain while seeking so strenuously to throw off the yoke of England that Tories in the settlements in which he was leader were hardly allowed the liberty of slaves. The extent of his sinning in the correspondence with Mero was to assure the Spaniard of the friendship of the people of the struggling Cumberland settlements, and in return for this he hoped to win Mero's good will to the extent of exercising an influence for peace over the Creeks and other hostile Indians.

Gen. Robertson continued to serve his people and the government ably and faithfully for many years after the State was admitted into the Union, and died "in harness." His death occurred at the Chickasaw Agency September 1, 1814. He was buried there, but in 1825 his remains were removed to Nashville and reinterred.

CHAPTER VII.

AN INTERESTING RECORD, TOGETHER WITH A TRAGEDY ON STONE'S RIVER.

Reference has been made to the erection of Donelson's station, on Stone's river, and to its subsequent abandonment. Also to the fact that Col. John Donelson, who founded the station, was to go to the Cumberland settlements by water, embarking at Fort Patrick Henry, on the Holston river.

Donelson's boat was called *The Adventure*, and carried a sail, while there were in addition several canoes and other craft. He kept an account of his trip, headed "Journal of a voyage intended by God's permission in the good boat *Adventure*, from Fort Patrick Henry, on Holston river, to the French Salt Springs, on the Cumberland river, kept by John Donelson." It has been preserved, and for clearness and directness is a model, and quite interesting, despite its lack of color. The diary is given entire:

December 22, 1779.—Took our departure from the fort and fell down the river to the mouth of Reedy creek, where we were stopped by the fall of water and most excessive hard frost; and after much delay and many difficulties, we arrived at the mouth of Cloud's creek, on Sunday evening, Feb. 20, 1780, where we lay until Sunday, the 27th, when we took our departure with sundry other vessels bound for the same voyage, and on the same day struck the Poor Valley Shoal, together with Mr. Boyd and Mr. Rounsifer, on which shoal we lay that afternoon and succeeding night in much distress.

Monday, February 28, 1780.—In the morning, the water rising, we got off the shoals after landing thirty persons to lighten our boat. In attempting to land on an island, received some damage, and lost sundry articles, and came to camp on the south shore, where we joined sundry other vessels also bound down.

Tuesday, 29th.—Proceeded down the river and encamped on the north shore, the afternoon and day following proving rainy.

Wednesday, March 1st.—Proceeded on, and encamped on the north shore, nothing happening that day very remarkable.

March 2.—Rain about half the day; passed the mouth of French Broad river, and about 12 o'clock Mr. Henry's boat, being drawn on the point of an island by force of the current, was sunk, the whole cargo much damaged, and the crew's lives much endangered, which occasioned the whole fleet to put on shore, and to go to their assistance, but with much difficulty baled her out and raised her, in order to take in her cargo again. The same afternoon Reuben Harrison went out a hunting, and did not return that night, though many guns were fired to fetch him in.

Friday, 3d.—Early in the morning fired a fourpounder for the lost man, sent out sundry persons to search the woods for him, firing many guns that day and the succeeding night, but all without success, to the great grief of his parents and fellow-travelers.

Saturday, 4th.—Proceeded on our voyage, leaving

A Dreary Voyage. 69

old Mr. Harrison, with some other vessels, to make further search for his lost son. About 10 o'clock the same day found him a considerable distance down the river, where Mr. Ben Belew took him on board his boat. At 3 o'clock p. m. passed the mouth of Tennessee river, and camped on the south shore, about ten miles below the mouth of the Tennessee.

Sunday, 5th.—Cast off and got under way before sunrise; 12 o'clock passed mouth of Clinch; at 3 o'clock p. m., came up with the Clinch river company, whom we joined, and camped, the evening proving rainy.

Monday, 6th.—Got under way before sunrise, the morning proving very foggy; many of the fleet were much bogged; about 10 o'clock lay by for them; when collected, proceeded down; camped on the north shore, where Capt. Hutching's negro man died, being much frosted in his feet and legs, of which he died.

Tuesday, 7th.—Got under way very early; the day proving windy, a S. S. W., and the river being wide, occasioned high sea, inasmuch that some of the smaller crafts were in danger; therefore came to at the uppermost Chickamauga town, which was then evacuated, where we lay by that afternoon and camped that night. A child was born to the wife of Ephraim Peyton. Mr. Peyton has gone through by land with Capt. Robertson.

Wednesday, 8th.—Cast off at 10 o'clock, and proceeded down to an Indian village, which was inhabited, on the south side of the river. They invited us to "come ashore," called us brothers, and showed other signs of friendship, insomuch that Mr. John Caffrey and my son, then on board, took a canoe, which I had in tow, and were crossing over to them, the rest of the fleet having landed on the opposite shore. After they had gone some distance, a half-breed, who called himself Archy Coody, with several other Indians, jumped into a canoe, met them, and advised them to return to the boat, which they did, together with Coody, and several canoes, which left the shore and followed directly after him. They appeared to be friendly. After distributing some presents among them, with which they seemed much pleased, we observed a number of Indians on the other side embarking in their canoes, armed and painted with red and black. Coody immediately made signs to his companions, ordering them to quit the boat, which they did, himself and another Indian remaining with us, and telling us to move off instantly. We had not gone far before we discovered a number of Indians armed and painted, proceeding down the river, as it were to intercept us. Coody, the half-breed, and his companion, sailed with us for some time, and, telling us that we had passed all the towns, and out of danger, left us. But we had not gone far until we came in sight of another town, situated likewise on the south side of the river, nearly opposite a small island. Here they again invited us to come on shore. called us brothers. and observing the boat's standing off for the opposite channel, told us that their side of the river was better for boats to pass. And here we must regret the unfortunate death of young Mr. Payne, on board Capt. Blackmore's boat, who was mortally wounded by reason of the boat running too near the northern shore, opposite the town where some of the enemy lay concealed, and the more tragical misfortune of poor Stuart, his family and friends, to the number of twenty-eight persons. This man had embarked with us for the western country, but his family being diseased with the smallpox, it was agreed upon between him and the company that he should keep at some distance in the rear. for fear of the infection spreading, and he was warned each night when the encampment should take place by the sound of a horn. After we had passed the town, the Indians having now collected to a considerable number, observing his helpless situation, singled off from the rest of the fleet, intercepted him, killed and took prisoners the whole crew, to the great grief of the whole company, uncertain how soon they might share the same fate; their cries were distinctly heard by those boats in the rear. We still perceived them marching down the river in considerable bodies, keeping pace with us until the Cumberland mountains withdrew them from our sight, when we were in hopes we had escaped them. We are now arrived at the place called Whirl, or Suck, where the river is compressed within less than half its common width above, by the Cumberland mountains, which jut on both sides. In passing through the upper part of these narrows, at a place described by Coody, which he termed the "boiling pot," a trivial incident had nearly ruined the expedition. One of the company, John Cotton, who was moving down in a large canoe, had attached it to Robert Cartwright's boat, into which he and his family had gone for safety. The canoe was here overturned, and the little cargo lost. The company, pitying his distress, concluded to halt and assist him in recovering his property. They had landed on the northern shore, at a level spot, and were going up to the place, when the Indians, to our astonishment, appeared immediately over us on the opposite cliffs, and commenced firing down upon us, which occasioned a precipitate retreat to the boats. We immediately moved off. The Indians, lining the bluff along, continued their fire from the heights on our boats below, without doing any other injury than wounding four slightly. Jennings' boat is missing.

We have now passed the Whirl. The river widens with a placid and gentle current, and all the company appear to be in safety, except the family of Jonathan Jennings, whose boat ran on a large rock projecting out from the northern shore, and partly immersed in water, immediately at the Whirl, where we were compelled to leave them, perhaps to be slaughtered by their merciless enemies. Continued to sail on that day, and floated throughout the following night.

Thursday, 9th.—Proceeded on our journey, nothing happening worthy of attention to-day; floated on until about midnight, and encamped on the northern shore.

Friday, 10th.—This morning about 4 o'clock we were surprised by the cries of, "Help poor Jennings!" at some distance in the rear. He had discovered us by our fires, and came up in the most wretched condition. He states that as soon as the Indians had discovered his situation, they turned their whole attention to him, and kept up a most galling fire on his boat. He ordered his wife, a son nearly grown, a young man who accompanied them, and his two negroes, to throw all his goods into the river, to lighten their boat for the purpose of getting her off, himself returning their fire, being a good soldier and an excellent marksman. But before they had accomplished their object, his son, the young man and the negro, jumped out of the boat and left him. He thinks the young man and the negro were wounded. Before they left the boat Mrs. Jennings, however, and the negro woman succeeded in unloading the boat, but chiefly by the exertions of Mrs. Jennings, who got out of the boat and shoved her off, but came near falling a victim to her intrepidity on account of the boat starting so suddenly as soon as loosened from the rocks. Upon examination he appears to have made a wonderful escape, for his boat is pierced in numberless places with bullets. It is to be remarked that Mrs. Peyton, to whom was born an infant the night before—which was unfortunately killed in the hurry and confusion consequent upon such a disaster—assisted them, being frequently exposed to wet and cold then and afterwards, and that her health appears to be good at this time, and I think and hope she will do well. Their clothes are very much cut with bullets, especially Mrs. Jennings'.

Saturday, 11th.—Got under way after having distributed the family of Mrs. Jennings in the other boats. Rowed on quietly that day, and encamped for the night on the northern shore.

Sunday, 12th.—Set out, and after a few hours' sailing we heard the crowing of cocks, and soon came within view of the town; here they (the Indians) fired on us again without doing any injury. After running until about 10 o'clock, came in sight of the Muscle Shoals. Halted on the northern shore at the upper end of the shoals, in order to search for the signs Capt. James Robertson was to make at that place. He set out from Holston early in the fall of 1779, and was to proceed by the way of Kentucky to the Big Salt Lick, on Cumberland river, with several others in company; was to come across from the Big Salt Lick to the upper end of the shoals, there to make signs that we might know he had been there, and that it was practicable for us to cross by land. But to our great mortification we can find none, from which we conclude that it would not be prudent to make the attempt, and are determined, knowing ourselves to be in such eminent danger, to pursue our journey down the river. After trimming our boats in the best manner possible, we ran through the shoals before night. When we approached them they had a dreadful appearance to those who had never seen them before. The water being high, made a terrible roaring, which could be heard at some distance among the driftwood heaped frightfully upon the points of the islands, the current running in every direction. Here we did not know how soon we should be dashed to pieces, and all our troubles ended at once. Our boats frequently dragged on the bottom, and appeared constantly in danger of striking; they warped as much as in a rough sea. But, by the hand of Providence, we are now preserved from this danger also. I know not the length of this wonderful shoal: it had been represented to me to be twenty-five or thirty miles; if so we must have descended very rapidly, as indeed we did, for we passed it in about three hours, came to and encamped on the northern shore, not far below the shoals, for the night.

Monday, 13th.—Got under way early in the morning and made a good run that day.

Tuesday, 14th.—Set out early. On this day two boats approaching too near the shore, were fired on by the Indians; five of the crew were wounded, but not dangerously. Came to camp at night near the mouth of a creek. After kindling fires and preparing for rest, the company were alarmed on account of the incessant barking our dogs kept up; taking it for granted the Indians were attempting to surprise us, we retreated precipitately to the boats, fell down the river about a mile, and encamped on the other shore. In the morning I prevailed on Mr. Caffrey and my son to cross below in a canoe, and return to the place, which they did, and found an African negro we had left in a hurry, asleep by one of the fires. The voyagers then returned and collected their utensils, which they had left.

Wednesday, 15th.—Got under way and moved on

peaceably on the five following days, when we arrived at the mouth of the Tennessee on Monday, 20th, and landed on the lower point, immediately on the bank of the Ohio. Our situation here is truly disagreeable. The river is very high and the current rapid; our boats not constructed for the purpose of stemming a rapid stream, our provisions exhausted, the crews almost worn down with hunger and fatigue, and know not what distance we have to go, or what time it will take us to our place of destination. The scene is rendered still more melancholy, as several boats will not attempt to ascend the rapid current. Some intend to descend the Mississippi to Natchez; others are bound for the Illinois—among the rest my son-in-law and daughter. We now part, perhaps to meet no more, for I am determined to pursue my course, happen what will.

Tuesday, 21st.—Set out, and on this day labored very hard, and got but a little way; camped on the south bank of the Ohio. Passed the two following days as the former, suffering much from hunger and fatigue.

Friday, 24th.—About 3 o'clock came to the mouth of a river which I thought was the Cumberland. Some of the company declared it could not be, it was so much smaller than was expected. But I never heard of any river running in between the Cumberland and Tennessee. It appeared to flow with a gentle current. We determined, however, to make the trial, pushed up some distance, and encamped for the night.

Saturday, 25th.—To-day we are much encouraged: the river grows wider; the current is very gentle; we are now convinced it is the Cumberland. I have derived great assistance from a small square sail, which was fixed up on the day we left the mouth of the river, and to prevent any ill-effects from sudden flaws of wind, a man was stationed at each of the lower corners of the sheet, with directions to give way whenever it was necessary.

Sunday, 26th.—Got under way early; procured some buffalo meat; though poor, it was palatable.

Monday, 27th.—Set out again; killed a swan, which was very delicious.

Tuesday, 28th.—Set out very early this morning; killed some buffalo.

Wednesday, 29th.—Proceeded up the river; gathered some herbs on the bottoms of Cumberland, which some of the company called "Shawnee salad."

Thursday, 30th.—Proceeded on our voyage. This day we killed some more buffalo.

Friday, 31st.—Set out this day, and, after running some distance, met with Col. Richard Henderson, who was running the line between Virginia and North Carolina. At this meeting we were much rejoiced. He gave us every information we wanted, and further informed us that he had purchased a quantity of corn in Kentucky to be shipped at the Falls of Ohio, for the use of the Cumberland settlement. We are now without bread, and are compelled to hunt the buffalo to preserve life. Worn out with fatigue, our progress at present is slow. Camped at night near the mouth of a little river, at which place and below there is a handsome bottom of rich land. Here we found a pair of hand millstones, set up for grinding, but appeared not to have been used for a great length of time. Proceeded on quietly until April 12, at which time we came to the mouth of a little river running in on the north side, by Moses Renfroe and his company called Red river, up which they intended to settle. Here they took leave of us. We proceeded up Cumberland, nothing happening material until the 23rd, when we reached the first settlement on the north side of the river, one mile and a half below the Big Salt Lick, and called Eaton's station, after a man of that name, who, with several other families, came through Kentucky and settled there.

Monday, April 24th.—This day we arrived at our journey's end at the Big Salt Lick, where we had the pleasure of finding Capt. Robertson and his company. It is a source of satisfaction to us to be enabled to restore to him and others their families and friends, who were entrusted to our care, and who some time since, perhaps, despaired of ever meeting again. Though our prospects at present are dreary, we have found a few log cabins which have been built on a cedar bluff above the lick by Capt Robertson and his company.

As a result of the capture of Stuart, narrated by Col. Donelson, the smallpox broke out among the Indians, killing hundreds. The decimation of the tribes by the disease, as well as the cold winters, may have been the cause of the immunity from savage outrages which the settlers experienced for awhile after reaching the Cumberland country.

Soon after his arrival at Nashborough, in 1780, Col. Donelson began to search for a suitable location. He passed up the west bank of the Cumberland to the mouth of Stone's river, thence up that stream until he reached what afterwards became widely known as the Clover Bottom, near the bridge, on the Lebanon and Nashville turnpike. Here he removed with his family and servants and erected some shanties. There was a great deal of open ground in the bottoms, covered with white clover; and these open places enabled him to get in his crop of corn in a very seasonable time. A strong fence was needed, as there were immense herds of buffalo and deer ranging through the forest; but Donelson's expectation was, in the absence of such enclosures, to watch and frighten them. This place was called Donelson's station.

Having planted his corn on the south side of the river, he planted some cotton on the north side. The crops were growing rapidly, but in July there were such heavy rains that the corn was covered by the river's overflow. In addition to this calamity, the Indians had already appeared on the Cumberland and killed some of the settlers. Col. Donelson at once decided to remove to Mansker's station.

He hunted out other lands after going to Mansker's, but it was too late to cast a crop and expect it to mature before frost. After awhile he decided to go to Kentucky, but before going he ascertained that his corn had not been damaged by the overflow at Donelson's, but had thrived and would yield abundantly. He generously proposed to divide this crop with the settlers at Nashborough, and of course the offer was accepted. A day was agreed upon to meet and gather the crop. The company from Nashborough was commanded by Abel Gower, and others of this party were Abel Gower, Jr., John Randolph Robertson, and seven or eight more men, white and black. That from Mansker's was under the direction of Capt. John Donelson, second son of Col. Donelson.

More Indian Butcheries. 79

They ascended Stone's river, and, fastening their boats to the bank, began gathering it and carrying it to the boats. They were engaged several days. During each night when they were in camp, their dogs kept up an incessant barking. It was suggested by some of the party that the dogs scented Indians in the surrounding woods. Others thought that as there was much fresh meat in the camp, and offal left in the woods where some buffalo had been killed, the wolves were attracted thereby, and the dogs were barking at them.

During the last night's encampment the dogs rushed out furiously in every direction around the camps. There were savages lurking in the woods, their stealthy movements undoubtedly influencing the dogs. As used as they were to the ruses of the Indians, perhaps the settlers heard but did not heed the hooting of an owl in the wood, or the bleat of a fawn, as the Indians signaled each other. And with culpable carelessness they made no examination next morning for Indian signs, but hastened the completion of their loads. Capt. Donelson crossed the river and began to pick the cotton north of the river, but Capt. Gower refused to be delayed by trying to save the cotton, and drifted down the river. He had not gone far, however, before the Indians, who were in ambush on the south side, apparently several hundred in number, opened fire on him and his men. Some of them were killed outright; others jumped out into the water and were tomahawked. The fact that any escaped the merciless fire is due to the fact that because of the scarcity of powder, the Indians always loaded lightly, and to the further fact that their guns were of a poor quality. The larger portion of the savages, too, were armed only with bows and arrows, and blow guns and arrows.

A white man and a negro escaped to the woods; another negro, Jack Civil, surrendered and was taken into captivity. The two who escaped wandered for about twenty hours, but finally reached the fort at Nashborough. John Randolph Robertson, a relative of James Robertson, was among the slain.

Capt. Donelson could see the attack from the cotton patch plainly. When the Indians fired he ran down to his boat and secured his rifle and ammunition. Rising the bank, he saw the Indians in pursuit of several men, those who had jumped from Gower's boat. He also discovered a body of savages making their way up stream opposite his boat. He fired at the party, and then rushed after his friends, who had fled into the cane on hearing the firing and yelling of the Indians.

After he had overtaken the fleeing party they agreed upon the direction to be separately taken, so that they might assemble the next day upon a bank of the Cumberland, above the mouth of Stone's river, where they would attempt to cross the river and reach Mansker's station. They then separated, to prevent making a trail that would lead the Indians.

The Escape.

Having traveled till sunset, Capt. Donelson discovered a large hickory tree which had fallen to the ground, its leaves not yet dropped. He called in the wanderers, and they huddled there all night in the cold November rain, without fire, the winds whistling through the trees, the rain dropping from the shaken foliage, the memory of the day's tragedy in their minds, and the wild voices of the wilderness in their ears.

They constructed a rude float the next morning and attempted to cross the river, but the current invariably drove them back; then Somerset, a faithful servant belonging to Capt. Donelson, volunteered to swim the river with the aid of a horse they had along, and ride to the station and solicit aid. The party, through the help of friends thus brought, finally reached the station. Further discouraged, Col. Donelson left soon afterward with his family for Kentucky.

At this time Col. Donelson's daughter, Rachel, who afterwards became the wife of Andrew Jackson, was a girl not yet arrived at womanhood.

CHAPTER VIII.

TERRITORIAL MATTERS, INCLUDING SOME OF THE PUBLIC ACTS OF WILLIAM BLOUNT.

Near the entrance to the cemetery of the First Presbyterian Church at Knoxville, there is a plain stone slab partially hidden by the rank growth of shrubbery, and containing the inscription: "William Blount. Died March 21, 1800. Aged 53 years." There is an air of neglect about the grave; for there is no one to care. The people of one generation easily forget those of a previous one. Those who knew and loved him also succumbed to the changes and ravages which have marked a century's going.

> "The mossy marbles rest
> On the lips that he has pressed
>   In their bloom;
> And the names he loved to hear
> Have been carved for many a year
>   On the tomb."

The idler pausing to glance at the old capitol not far off, with its gray walls and dingy little windows, may for a moment recall the name and career of this once popular man whose best years were given to Tennessee, but who now sleeps beneath the plain slab with

A New Territory. 83

the simple inscription. He recalls the period in which Blount was governor, his friendship before that for the first settlers of the State, and his impeachment and expulsion from the United States Senate; and then matters of to-day exile the thoughts of "old, unhappy, far-off things, and battles long ago."

On February 25, 1790, Benj. Hawkins and Samuel Johnston, members of the United States Senate from North Carolina, signed the deed of cession which made Tennessee a territory of the United States; the act of acceptance was approved April 2; and on May 26, 1790, an act was passed for its government. William Blount, an intimate friend of Washington and a popular person among the people of the new territory, was appointed governor; David Campbell became judge; and Daniel Smith was made secretary. On recommendation of the governor John Sevier and James Robertson became brigadier-generals of Washington and Mero Districts respectively. The three leading features of Gov. Blount's administration, as one writer correctly remarks, were the contests with the Indians, the gradual extinguishment of their title to lands in the limits of the present State, and the final triumph of America in the diplomatic contests with Spain.

He was, in addition to being governor of the territory, appointed superintendent of Indian affairs, embracing the four Southern tribes, the Cherokees, Creeks, Choctaws and Chickasaws. His superintendency bordered upon the frontiers of Virginia, North Carolina.

South Carolina, Georgia and Kentucky and Tennessee, within the boundaries of which the Southern tribes resided or claimed hunting grounds. There were constant collisions between the whites and Indians; and all complaints between these parties were cognizable by and made to him for redress. His duties were therefore arduous as well as delicate, and it cannot be gainsaid that in these affairs he displayed unusual administrative capacity. He was decidedly the man for the position.

In his efforts to bring about peace between the Indians and the United States, it was often necessary to meet the savages in treaty. The particulars of the occurrences of one of these meetings are given by Ramsey. In 1791 he sent through Maj. King and others to the Cherokee chiefs to meet him in a peace talk. The point of meeting was four miles below the confluence of the Holston and French Broad rivers. Gov. Blount received and entertained there the chiefs and head warriors with marked ceremonies. It may be inferred that his part was carried out perfectly, when we reflect that—to quote Phelan—"he had perhaps caught something of the Old World elegance from the foreign element which in those days thronged our larger cities, and was himself on occasions as stately, dignified, and courtly as any of those who frequented the *salons* of Paris, to pay light compliments to Madame Recamier or to laugh at the saturnine witticisms of the Encyclopedists." The treaty ground was on the site of Knoxville. The gov-

ernor appeared in full dress, and wore a sword and
military hat, trappings which impress the Indian always.
He remained seated near his marquee, under the tall
trees which shaded the Holston. His officers, civil and
military, stood near, uncovered and respectful. Behind
the officials in groups stood the citizens and strangers
attracted by the occasion; the soldiery were not present.
James Armstrong, who had seen service in Europe and
was familiar with foreign etiquette, presented each Indian to the governor after the interpreter had introduced him to Armstrong. Forty-one Indians were introduced, in order according to their age, and not after
their rank. The delegation was very large; there were
twelve hundred Indians, including women and children.
The warriors were decorated with eagle feathers on
their heads and other insignia, but were unarmed; the
older chiefs and wise men wore the common Indian
dress only. After the presentation was over, the governor opened the conference through the interpreter;
and during its continuance the Indians observed their
own council-house tactics—that is to say, the speaker
alone standing, while his colleagues sat upon the ground
in a circle around him in respectful silence, but strictly
attentive.

But despite Gov. Blount's efforts to secure peace, his
object was not readily attained. During his administration Gen. Sevier, Col. Doherty, Col. Beard and others
were kept busy protecting the eastern settlements from
the Indians, and in attacking and destroying their

towns. So continuous had the depredations become that even the governor half-way decided that the destruction of their towns alone would insure immunity.

In 1793, however, a series of outrages brought about such a castigation from the whites as promised respite at last. John Watts and Double Head, two resolute Indian chiefs, at the head of a body of a thousand Cherokee and Creek warriors, decided to attack Knoxville, then a very small station, having in view, perhaps, the stores at that place. On the evening of September 24, they crossed the Tennessee river below the mouth of the Holston. The army presented a formidable appearance, with seven hundred painted Creeks, one hundred being mounted, and three hundred Cherokees, each individual actuated by the most savage instincts. They marched all night, hoping to reach Knoxville before day, but a delay at the river prevented this. The delay, Ramsey says, was due mainly to an altercation between the leaders. "Knoxville being the principal object of attack and plunder," he continues, "orders were given by some of the Creeks to press forward at once, and not delay their march by stopping to disturb and plunder the smaller settlements. Double Head advised a different policy, and insisted on taking every cabin as they passed. A further cause of delay was the rivalry between this chief and Van, each of whom aspired to the leadership of the expedition. Upon the question, 'Shall we massacre all the inhabitants of Knoxville, or the men only?' these savage warriors differed in opinion; Van advising leniency to the women and children. Before the plan of procedure was adjusted, the night was so far spent as not to allow the invaders time to reach Knoxville before daylight. By dawn they were in a few miles of their object of attack, and were marching rapidly, when the United States troops at Knoxville, as was their custom, fired a cannon at sunrise. The Indians supposed from this that they were expected, and abandoned the attack."

When they halted, they espied not far off the station of Alexander Cavet, protected by three gun-men only. It was located about eight miles from Knoxville. The Indians determined to attack it. The three inmates made the best defense possible, killing a Creek and a Cherokee, and wounding three more. Strange to say, the Indians were held at bay for some time by the spirited defense. They then sent Bob Benge, a halfbreed, with a proposal that if the station were surrendered, its inmates should not be killed. The terms were accepted. As the whites left the house, they were attacked by Double Head and others, and were all killed and mutilated with the exception of Alexander Cavet, Jr., a lad. He was spared through the interposition of Watts, only to be killed later in one of the Indian towns. It should be stated to the credit of Benge that he did all in his power to save the victims after their capitulation.

The savage horde marched in the direction of Clinch river, and Gen. Sevier began at once making preparations to invade the Indian country. His army with all reinforcements numbered six or seven hundred mounted men. Here, too, was a formidable array of fighting men, quite as much so as that which appeared a few days before under the command of Watts and Double Head; determined mountaineers with their long rifles and undaunted spirits; grizzled Indian fighters and younger men who could be as certainly depended upon; earlier-day Rough Riders who had long before discarded such feelings as fear.

Crossing the Little Tennessee, after a rapid march they reached Estimaula, an Indian village, where they secured a supply of grain and meat. They burned the town, and camped in its immediate vicinity on Estimaula river. Sentries were placed around the camp, for a night attack was expected; and the horses were tethered where they would be safest.

The men lay upon their arms. They were tired, and knew they had vigilant sentries; and were gradually wrapped in slumber. An ominous stillness pervaded the camp, broken now and then by the heavy breathing of some sleeper, or the fretful cry of one of the Indian children captured at Estimaula. Presently the sentries heard a suspicious movement; Indians were approaching a few hundred yards away, in a slow, uniform manner, creeping through the yellow sage. They drew nearer and nearer—so close, that the cocking of their guns was heard. Firing, the sentries retired; and the Indians fired their guns also, at the same time making the woods ring with their war-whoops.

The camp was aroused, and there was enough confusion to allow the escape of some of the captive squaws and children. The Indians soon withdrew. The next night, Sevier took up his line of march to Etowah, an Indian town situated near the confluence of the Etowah and Coosa, and just across the former stream from the troops. By mistake the guides led the whites to a ferry below the ford, immediately opposite the town. Some of the men crossed to the farther bank, but the greater part pushed to the ford, intending to attack the town from that direction.

The mistake of the guides proved fortunate. The approach of the whites was apprehended, and the Indians had made excavations in the bank commanding the ford, each large enough for one man to lie with his gun poised. But thinking from the movement of the horsemen down the river that the attack would be made there, the warriors left their excavations and hurried down to defend the town. When they saw their mistake, it was too late to regain the pits; in addition to this, they became greatly scattered. The larger portion found themselves between the river and the whites; but they made a stubborn resistance under the leadership of Kingfisher. Hugh L. White, afterwards prominent as a statesman, and a few others resolved to kill this chief. When he fell under their unerring aim, the warriors gave up the fight and fled.

The village—which stood near the present town of Rome, Georgia—was burned. Sevier wanted to carry the war further down to other Indian settlements, but it was decided to return on account of the difficulties to be surmounted in reaching them.

The Etowah campaign was the last military service of Gen. Sevier. Although he had been the protection of the frontiers for nearly a score of years, fighting thirty-five battles and never meeting defeat, and in all his engagements losing but fifty-six men, this expedition was the only one for which he received compensation from the government. Commenting on his manner of warfare, Ramsey says that Sevier was the first to introduce the Indian war-whoop in his battles with the savages, the tories, or the British. More harmless than the leaden missile, it was not less efficient, and was always the precursor and attendant of victory. The prisoners at King's Mountain said, "We could stand your fighting, but your cursed hallooing confused us; we thought the mountains had regiments instead of companies."

The fall of Etowah practically put an end to Indian outrages in East Tennessee. In the more western settlements on the Cumberland the people still suffered throughout the greater part of Gov. Blount's administration; but through the determination of Gen. Robertson, as will be seen, the Nickojack expedition was undertaken and carried out, resulting in comparative peace to those long-suffering settlers.

BASIS FOR IMPEACHMENT. 91

When the territory came to an end and Tennessee became a State in 1796, Gov. Blount was elected as one of the senators of the United States from the new commonwealth. He and the other senator, William Cocke, were not allowed to take their seats owing to irregularities attending the first election laws of the State. They were later re-elected and repaired to Philadelphia.

While acting in his capacity of senator, Blount was impeached by the House of Representatives, being charged with high crimes and misdemeanors supposed to have been committed while a senator of the United States. The allegations were based on a letter to James Carey. Referring to this letter, Gen. Robertson once said: "I never could have judged the letter to have been so criminal, but supposed it would have operated against my friend, as being a public man." In 1797 Senator Blount wrote as follows to one of his constituents:

PHILADELPHIA, July 5, 1797.
In a few days you will see published by order of Congress, a letter said to have been written by me to James Carey. It makes quite a fuss here. I hope, however, the people upon the Western waters will see nothing but good in it, for so I intended, especially for Tennessee.

Whether the suggestion by Blount in the Carey letter justified or not the charge that he had "conspired to set on foot a military hostile expedition against the territory of his Catholic majesty in the Floridas and Louisiana for the purpose of wresting them from his Catholic majesty, and of conquering the same for Great Britain," he was on July 8 expelled from his seat. He returned to Knoxville, where he was welcomed, though disgraced. The sergeant-at-arms of the United States, James Matthers, followed him with the intention of arresting and carrying him in custody to the seat of government. Arriving at Knoxville, he found that the ex-senator had friends who thought him persecuted and misunderstood; and that whatever the feeling in Philadelphia was, the Western people retained confidence in the man who had been a tried and true friend in their service for many years. Matthers was for some days the guest of Blount, and was treated with politeness and even marked attention by the citizens of Knoxville. But when served with process, the ex-senator refused to go to Philadelphia. Matthers summoned a *posse* to his assistance—but not a person came to his aid; and when he started on his return to the seat of government, a number of citizens went with him a few miles from town and politely but firmly informed him that Blount could never be taken from Tennessee as a prisoner.

On January 14, 1799, judgment was pronounced by the Vice President that "the court is of opinion that the matter alleged in the plea of the defendant is sufficient in law to show that this court ought not to hold jurisdiction of the said impeachment, and that the said impeachment be dismissed." But before this announcement of the failure to sustain the prosecution, the people of his section had shown their confidence in Blount in a more substantial manner than in their treatment of Matthers. Blount was elected to the State Senate, and made speaker in 1798.

As in the case of Andrew Johnson, prejudice may have had much to do in the impeachment of Blount; or if it was not prejudice, it may have been an over-zealous desire of easily-frightened statesmen to prevent a rupture with Spain, then considerably more powerful than a century later. Like Andrew Johnson, too, he was as popular with his constituency after his impeachment as before. But he did not live long to enjoy their renewed tokens of esteem.

CHAPTER IX.

THE NICKOJACK EXPEDITION, WHICH RESULTED IN BREAKING THE SPIRIT OF THE INDIANS.

The selling into bondage of the favorite son of Jacob in the earlier history of the Hebrews seemed a misfortune to the father and youth, but it proved a blessing to the chosen people; and the hardships of Wallace's fictitious hero, Ben Hur—fitting him to successfully carry out the duties to devolve upon him—are but a repetition of a lesson as old as the ages. In April, 1788, Joseph Brown, a lad of sixteen years of age, was passing with his father and others in a boat down the Tennessee river on their way to the Cumberland settlements. The boat was captured by the Indians near Running Water town, and the crew butchered with a few exceptions. Among the captives was the lad mentioned. He was held by the Indians for several months, until their haunts became as well known to him as the neighborhood where he was reared. He was finally exchanged through the efforts of Sevier, an Indian squaw predicting at the time of the exchange that he would one day lead back an expedition for the destruction of the Indians. This prediction proved true.

ORE GIVEN COMMAND.

When Indian raids on the Cumberland people became so intolerable that Gen. Robertson resolved, despite the warnings of the territorial governor, William Blount, and the instructions of the general government, to make an attack on Nickojack, Running Water and other Indian towns, Brown was selected to discover a route thereto and guide the expedition, the circumstance emphasizing the idea of disguised blessings once more. Troops were raised in Kentucky through the efforts of Sampson Williams, of the Cumberland settlements; Col. Ford levied others between Nashville and Clarksville on the east side of Cumberland river; Col. Montgomery joined the force with a company from Clarksville; while Gen. Robertson raised volunteers in and around Nashville. Maj. Ore, who had been ordered with a command of mounted men to protect Mero District, arrived at Nashville while the expedition was being projected, and on September 6, 1794, was given command by Gen. Robertson in an explicit and yet ingeniously-worded order.

On the next day the army marched to the Black Fox's camp where Murfreesboro now stands; next day it crossed Duck river near the stone fort at Manchester; then crossing Elk river and Cumberland Mountain it reached the Tennessee about three miles below the mouth of Sequatchee. An encampment was made there as it was night when they arrived. Before dawn of the following day the army was busily engaged crossing the river, and began a cautious march up the mountain between the point of which and the river Brown and Richard Finnelson, the guides, said the town of Nickojack lay. The troops under Ore numbered over five hundred, according to Ore's official report, and they reached the town on September 13.

Nickojack was inhabited by two or three hundred Indians. They consisted mainly of bandits. Of the topographical features of Nickojack and Running Water a historian remarks: "The situation of these towns caught a certain air of picturesque gandeur from the natural scenery around them. The two most important were Nickojack and Running Water. They were situated on a precipice which was all but impregnable. A deep, broad, dangerous river ran below. Beyond were the dense forests, penetrated only by the paths which successive generations of wild beasts had made, and the tall, inaccessible peaks of the Cumberland Mountains, down whose dark and precipitous ravines it was supposed no horse could ever descend. The approach in the rear was impossible to all but friends. The eagle in his eerie, the panther in his lair, could not be safer."

The spot was indeed an ideal one for the fierce Chickamaugas and their few white associates. It was a little world to itself. After a descent upon the settlements, the warriors could return there, bid anxiety depart, and enjoy the fruits of their plunderings; there the women might watch their offspring gamboling in the sunshine without fear of the intrusion of an enemy.

NICKOJACK VILLAGE. 97

For years they had enjoyed immunity. In the spring the birds trilled their poems of peace; in the summer the woods were green and the waters clear, and cloud-shadows passing over the mountains were not an augury even to those superstitious beings of coming disasters; when autumn came with its haze, and red, gold and green tints, and that wonderful pathos in the air for things passing away, did not nature still hold eternal guard and assure them that there were none to molest or make afraid?

But the sense of perfect safety is not infrequently but a moment's distance from doom. Maj. Ore's troops were divided into two wings—the main body under Col. Whitley was to make a detour and attack Nickojack above, while the other wing, under Montgomery, was to attack below. So great was the Indians' feeling of security that no sentries were posted at the approaches to the town, and the whites were upon them and shooting them down before they knew the foe was within a hundred miles of those fastnesses. Two houses were seen in the cornfields about two hundred and fifty feet from the village. To prevent their discovery by the Indians in time to make a defense, the troops rushed in full speed in the direction of Nickojack. They passed the cabins, which were found to be vacant, and hastened to the landing on the river where the fleeing savages were endeavoring to escape in their canoes. Besides three or four boat loads in the river, there were twenty-five or thirty warriors standing on the bank.

William Pillow, who was in the lead of the whites, fired at them, and his shot was followed by a destructive volley from Col. Montgomery's force, which left hardly an Indian alive. A few, however, escaped by covering themselves with the plunder in the canoes or by diving. Col. Whitley, who was above the town, sent Brown back with a detachment of about twenty men to intercept those Indians who might try to escape from the mouth of the creek which emptied into the river below. Then Whitley and his command rushed down. The Indians were helplessly hemmed, and their destruction was thorough.

Running Water was four miles higher up the river. After destroying Nickojack, the troops marched to that place. Its inhabitants had fled, and the whites, after razing the village, which was larger than Nickojack, began their homeward march. The other villages were unimportant, and Maj. Ore decided to leave them unmolested. Maj. Ore's report to Gov. Blount is interesting, and is therefore given here:

KNOXVILLE, September 24, 1794.

SIR: On the seventh instant, by order of Gen. Robertson, of Mero District, I marched from Nashville with five hundred and fifty mounted infantry under my command, and pursued the trace of the Indians who had committed the latest murders in the District of Mero, and of the party that captured Peter Turney's negro woman to the Tennessee. I crossed it on the night of the twelfth, about four miles below Nickojack, and in the morning of the thirteenth, destroyed Nicko-

Major Ore's Report.

jack and Running Water, towns of the Cherokees. The first being entirely surrounded and attacked by surprise, the slaughter was great, but cannot be accurately reported, as many were killed in the Tennessee. Nineteen women and children were made prisoners at this town. The Running Water town being only four miles above Nickojack, the news of the attack upon the latter reached the former before the troops under my command, and a resistance was made to save it at a place called the Narrows; but, after the exchange of a few rounds, the Indians posted at that place gave way, and the town was burnt without further opposition, with all the effects found therein, and the troops under my command recrossed the Tennessee the same day. From the best judgment that could be formed, the number of Indians killed at the towns must have been upwards of fifty, and the loss sustained by the troops under my command, was one lieutenant and two privates wounded.

Running Water was counted the largest and among the most hostile towns of the Cherokees. Nickojack was not less hostile, but inferior in point of numbers. At Nickojack were found two fresh scalps which had lately been taken at Cumberland, and several that were old were hanging in the houses of the warriors, as trophies of war; a quantity of ammunition, powder and lead, lately arrived there from the Spanish government, and a commission for the Breath, the head man of the town, who was killed, and sundry horses and other articles of property, were found both at Nickojack and Running Water, which were known by one or other of the militia to have belonged to different people killed by the Indians in the course of the last twelve months.

The prisoners taken, among whom was the wife and child of Richard Finnelson, my pilot, informed me that, on the fourth instant, sixty Creeks and Lower Cherokees passed the Tennessee for war against the frontiers. They also informed me that two nights before the destruction of Running Water a scalp dance had been held in it over the scalps lately taken from Cumberland, at which were present John Watts, the Bloody Fellow and the other chiefs of the lower towns, and at which they determined to continue the war, in conjunction with the Creeks, with more activity than heretofore against the frontiers of the United States, and to erect block-houses at each of the lower towns for their defense, as advised by the Spanish government. The prisoners also informed me that a scalp-dance was to be held in two nights at Redheaded Will's town, a new town about thirty miles lower down the Tennessee.

The troops under my command generally behaved well.

I have the honor to be your excellency's most obedient, humble servant.

JAMES ORE.

Gov. BLOUNT.

Joseph Brown, the guide, had a talk with an Indian at Tellico block-house after the expedition, in which he was informed that the loss of the enemy at the destruction of Nickojack was seventy instead of fifty.

Thoughtful and fair people who understand the situation in Mero District at that time, will agree that the invasion of the Indian country was necessary for the peace and safety of the people, and that the government's policy of submission to Indian outrages was criminally erroneous. But notwithstanding this, Gen. Robertson was censured by the government and rebuked by Gov. Blount. The fact that he knew that he was justified by his own people, who were in a position to know the state of affairs in the district, doubtless caused him to lose little sleep over what Haywood expresses as governmental snarling.

Comparative freedom from Indian annoyances was the result of the Nickojack expedition.

The people of Mero District were occasionally harassed by murders and thefts, and kept scouts among the settlements until the Creek wars; but the fears and real dangers of former days were forever gone. The approach of the second war with England somewhat stimulated the Indians' hopes of resisting the broadening sway of the Americans, but their efforts did not seriously disturb the Tennessee settlements.

From the first settlement at Watauga in 1768 to the admission of Tennessee into the Union, the whites had withstood a savage horde estimated at something like one hundred and fifty thousand, of whom twenty thousand were warriors—immediate neighbors of the settlers; while beyond the Mississippi was an unknown myriad in friendly alliance with the other savages. Their perseverance and courage prevailed in the end, however.

CHAPTER X.

MERE GLIMPSES OF CERTAIN OTHER CHARACTERS FIGURING IN THE EARLY SETTLEMENTS.

A decidedly prominent and daring pioneer of the eastern section in its incipient settlement was James Hubbard, who lived at Watauga. His parents had been murdered when he was a boy, and the passion of his life appeared to be to avenge their massacre. He possessed absolute coolness in danger, as well as the cunning of the craftiest savage. It is said that he could practice, and had practiced for years, and successfully, the strategies of single-handed warfare, and excelled the boldest and shrewdest of the race he hated. The Indians knew him and feared him more than any man of his time, not excepting perhaps Simon Kenton and Daniel Boone. While he possessed their courage and skill, he was lacking in pity, for his hatred of the Indians could not be softened by any appeal to his conscience.

The Indians for some time before the establishment of the State of Franklin had been subjecting the East Tennessee settlements to their customary annoyances, and the lethargic attitude of North Carolina toward Indian atrocities on the frontier was one thing which suggested to the pioneers the idea of a separate government—one which would insure greater protection. No doubt the Indians had some cause for provocation. It was alleged by them, and believed by the governor of North Carolina, that the killing of an Indian chief by Hubbard was one motive for Indian hostility. The facts of the chief's death are as follows: He was known as Butler by the whites, as Untoola by the Indians. In a fight with Hubbard once he had been disarmed and sent back to his tribe without weapons, and consequently disgraced. The chief smarted under this disgrace, and naturally cherished the hope of revenge. Sometime after this occurrence, and while a sort of peace was patched up between the Cherokees of the upper towns and the whites, corn became scarce among the latter. They sent among the Indians for supplies, and Hubbard, going on one of these missions despite the aversion with which the savages regarded him, selected the village where Butler had been a chief. Perhaps he was actuated by a desire to aggravate his already mortified and discomfited enemy.

Butler learned of Hubbard's approach, and going out with a friend to meet him, asked why he had come there. This was said with an air of insult, but Hubbard showed an empty corn sack, and explained that he had come to purchase corn. He then offered the two Indians a drink of whiskey. The disgraced chief made no reply, but stood looking with hate on his ancient enemy. Not the least disturbed, but apparently desirous of peace, Hubbard leaned his gun against a tree and returned the gaze of the Indian; but when he noticed Butler ride toward him, with the intention of getting between him and his gun, he laid his hand upon the muzzle. The Indian struck at him, and missed; then raising his gun, fired. Dodging his head adroitly, he escaped, though the bullet cut a scar in his temple. The two Indians turned and tried to escape, but had not gotten more than eighty yards off when Hubbard shot Butler from his horse. The latter was not killed by the shot, and Hubbard picked him up and leaned him against a tree. This would doubtless have been the end of the difficulty, but Butler taunted him until the now enraged white broke his skull with his rifle barrel. With his usual good fortune, Hubbard escaped.

Another tragedy in which he figured was characterized by his dominant heartlessness where the Indians were concerned. In the early months of 1788 the Cherokees began to yearn for war. Their first hostile act of the year was a massacre which causes the blood to curdle at its mention. A family of the name of Kirk lived on the southwest side of Little river, twelve miles south of the present city of Knoxville. In May, the head of the family and a son were called away from home. During their absence an Indian, familiarly known as Slim Tom, who had been apparently a friend of the Kirks, came to the house and requested some provisions. The hospitable family readily supplied him. While there, he took especial cognizance of the surroundings, and seeing that the whites were not prepared for a defense, withdrew to the woods. Soon afterwards he returned with a party of his race, and massacred the eleven members of the family, leaving them dead in the yard.

It was a fearful instance of ingratitude, but it entailed a retaliation that was as horrifying.

When Kirk returned to his home, he was greeted with the sight of his family brutally murdered, lying with mutilated forms under the blue skies of his adopted land. He gave the alarm, and the militia gathered under John Sevier to the number of several hundred, and several Indian towns were burned and a great number of savages killed. But during the raid, the murder of the Kirk family was shockingly avenged in a way which, notwithstanding the provocation, cannot be condoned. A friendly Indian, Abraham, had refused to go to war with his people. In this resolution he met the indorsement of his son. The two lived on the north side of the Tennessee, and when the troops of Sevier arrived on the south side, Hubbard sent for Abraham and his son to come over. They came, doubtless believing that their friendship would be met with the gratitude it merited. Hubbard then, while Sevier was absent and not suspecting that a tragedy was to be enacted, ordered them to return and bring The Tassel and another Indian that he might have a talk with them. Some half a dozen Indians were brought to the troops in this way, and were confined in a house contiguous.

Hubbard, accompanied by a son of the settler, Kirk, whose family had been butchered on Little River, was allowed to go into the room where the Indians were confined, the troops, it is averred, being aware of the cause for the visit. Kirk deliberately walked up to one of the prisoners, and sunk his tomahawk into his skull, the Indian falling dead at his feet.

The other Indians by this time comprehending the situation, realized what would be their fate, but they did not murmur. Their demeanor should have disarmed the two men's hatred and led them to spare the guiltless. The scene which occurred in the Roman senate of old, when the savage invaders entered it, was in a measure re-enacted, though the victims in this instance showed the dignity and fortitude of the representatives of civilization in the first. Casting their glance on the ground, the Indians without a murmur awaited death. Kirk struck each on the upper part of the head with his tomahawk, killing all before he stopped.

"Sevier, returning, saw the tragical effects of this rash act," says Haywood, "and, on remonstrating against it, was answered by Kirk who was supported by some of the troops, that if he had suffered from the murderous hands of the Indians, as he (Kirk) had, he (Sevier) would have acted in the same way. Sevier, unable to punish him, was obliged to overlook the flagitious deed and acquiesce in the reply."

There can be no doubt about Hubbard instigating this affair. Strange to relate, despite his merciless enmity toward the Indians, he was not a terror to his own people, but was considered a valuable man in the needs of frontier life.

Reference is made in another chapter to Thomas Sharpe Spencer, the giant, who was the earliest settler of Middle Tennessee. Writers of the State's annals agree in pronouncing him one of the bravest of men, an ideal frontiersman. When he came to the section which he afterwards made his home, he was accompanied by other hunters, but they soon left. He spent the winter of 1779 and 1780 alone in the wilderness, taking up his abode in a hollow tree standing near the present site of Castalian Springs, Sumner County. The trunk of this tree was still visible just above ground in the first quarter of the nineteenth century, measuring twelve feet in circumference.

Miles Darden, a Tennessean, is said to have been the largest man on record, weighing a few years before his death over a thousand pounds. Probably Spencer did not approach him in size and weight, but he was of immense stature.

Stories are told of his prodigious strength that would astonish the public of to-day, familiar as it is with professional strong men. Amongst his courageous deeds is that of saving the life of Mrs. Bledsoe, wife of the Indian fighter and surveyor, Anthony Bledsoe. They were going through the country horseback, when they were fired upon by the Indians. Mrs. Bledsoe was thrown from her horse, and was in jeopardy of her life when Spencer took her up while the Indians' bullets were whistling around them, and reached a place of safety with her.

Spencer was finally slain by the savages on what is now Spencer's Hill, between Carthage and Crab Orchard, in 1794. He seemed to have no sense of fear of the Indians, often roaming and hunting alone in the forest for ten or twelve days at a time during the worst seasons of savage warfare.

Music may be said to be as essential to the enjoyment of mankind as sugar in some form is necessary to the system; and next to vocal music, that of the violin has been most highly appreciated by infant and primitive communities. In the backwoods to-day, fiddlers are more common than the performers on any other instrument. This was the case on the Tennessee frontier. A celebrated fiddler of early times has been given to posterity by Putnam. He was James Gamble. Paganini had a world-wide reputation as a violinist, and audiences went into ecstasies over his strains. Gamble's clientele was smaller; but as he went his way, enjoying life as Tennyson in one of his lyrics desired to do, "and fiddled in the timber," his performances were sufficient for the humble pioneers. He was the violinist of the Cumberland settlements, making his home at Bledsoe's station. He was a good-natured, happy man, making no enemies, and his wife appeared to enjoy his reputation notwithstanding the fact that he was so much wedded to his fiddle. "When the great revival came," says Putnam in his quaint tribute, "the dancing, involuntary and without ease or grace, continued; but instrumental music was condemned as unsuitable, and, indeed, sinful to be practiced or heard by professors of religion, and several of the fiddlers of Mero laid their instruments on the shelves or among old trumpery, and a few broke them in pieces. James Gamble (we hope) was also a Christian, a devotee to his science of sweet sounds upon horse-hair and catgut, but never a bigot. He read his Bible, and fiddled; he prayed, and he fiddled; asked a silent blessing on his meals, gave thanks, and fiddled; went to meeting, sang the songs of Zion, joined in all devotional services, went home, and fiddled. He sometimes fiddled in bed, but always fiddled when he got up. We doubt not he indulged in fiddling to excess, but if all men were as innocent of harm and contributed as much to the pleasure of their fellows as he, the world would be better than it is."

By dispensing his music, did not this backwoodsman scatter sunshine where it was most needed? Perhaps even his career impresses the fact that it is better to succeed in a humble sphere, doing well that of which we are capable, than to reflect little honor in a more important station.

Some men have given their talents and best efforts to win notoriety, and failed, or are only kept in remembrance by a song or a smart saying. Others without aspiration or effort or merit have had their memories strangely enough kept green, in a local sense, at least. Of the latter class was David Hood. He lived among the Nashborough people, and was a cooper; a simple, easy-going, garrulous person, given to garbling Scripture, and a tireless if tiresome punster.

There is something which appeals to our sense of the ludicrous in contemplating the occurrence which gave him his claim to recollection notwithstanding the horrible circumstances surrounding it. In the winter of 1782 he was returning from one of the nearby stations to Nashborough, when he was chased by a number of Indians, who fired as they pursued. Thinking that there was little chance to save his life in any event, he decided to make them believe he had been killed by one of their shots, and so fell on his face. In the language of the day, "possuming" was the word for feigning. When the Indians reached him one of them twisted his fingers in his hair, and scalped him. They then proceeded toward the fort he had tried to reach. When they had passed out of sight, their victim, bleeding but thankful that matters were no worse, got up and also started in the direction of Nashborough. Mounting the ridge above the sulphur spring, he was dismayed to see that the Indians had again discovered him. He turned to run, while the enemy fired shot after shot at him. One bullet struck him in the breast, but did not at once disable him. Bleeding profusely from his wound, he finally fell exhausted and unconscious in the snow. The Indians, after having inflicted what they considered mortal wounds, left him where he had fallen on a brush heap in the snow.

When found, Hood was taken to the fort and placed in an out-house as a dead man; but next morning some of the females, suggesting that life might not be quite extinct, expressed a desire to look at him. They thought they could perceive signs of life, and accordingly had him removed to better quarters. His wounds were dressed and cordials administered, and it was not long before his condition was encouraging. His convalescence was remarkably fast and it was but a few days until his native humor asserted itself in a pun as to having so completely "hoodwinked the Indians!"

Of the many locally-noted settlers, hunters and Indian fighters of the Cumberland country but one or two others will be mentioned. A volume might easily be devoted to the daring exploits of Anthony Bledsoe, John Rains, Spencer and Jonathan Jennings, Samson Williams, Casper Mansker and Abe Castleman. Castleman was an intimate friend of James Robertson, and had remained with him through all the vicissitudes of the new settlement. He had a perfectly trained ear. He could easily distinguish the report of the guns of the whites from that of the Indians. If a gun were fired in his hearing, he could even say whether it was Mansker's "Nancy" or the rifle of some other settler. When he went out to search for signs of Indians, the settlers could rely on his report, no matter how dim the trail. Mohammed could walk across a sand-bar and leave no track; Castleman could pass through the trackless woods as noiselessly as a cat creeping upon its prey. He could distinguish between the hoot of the owl and the best imitation. If the least uncertain, he was cautious enough to take no risks, though he never neglected an opportunity to satisfy himself, so great was his passion for adventure, so little did he regard danger. He gave one instance where he was not quite satisfied with his judgment. "It was in the dusk of the evening," said he. "The imitation of the large bird of night was very perfect, yet I was suspicious. The woo-woo call and the woo-woo answer were not well-timed and toned, and the babel-chatter was a failure; and more than this, I am sure they are on the ground, and that won't begin to do. 'I'll see you,' says I to myself, and as I approached, I saw something of the height of a stump standing between a forked tree which divided near the ground. Well, I know there can be no stump there; I put 'Betsy' to my face—that stump was once a live Indian, and he lay at the roots of those forked chestnuts. And if he was ever buried, it was not far off."

Among the tragedies enacted almost daily in 1793, his immediate relatives did not escape butchery. To retaliate, in August of that year he raised a number of volunteers, resolving to make a little incursion. Ten of his comrades turned back after reaching the Tennessee in pursuit of Indians, as Gen. Robertson prohibited scouting parties from crossing it. Castleman with only five others, all dressed and painted as Indians, crossed the river below Nickojack, the celebrated Indian town, and continued their still-hunt. They followed the trace leading to Will's Town, several miles below. Traveling ten or twelve miles, they discovered an Indian camp. It was composed of forty or fifty Creeks—a war party on the way to plunder the settlements. The Indians were eating, and as Castleman's men were disguised, mistook them for friends. Castleman was called the "Fool Warrior" by all the Indians who knew of his recklessness, and his temerity in this instance proved that the sobriquet was somewhat applicable. The whites were more than a hundred miles from home, in strange woods, and greatly out-numbered.

The party approached the Indians; then pausing when within a few paces of the camp, raised their guns and fired. Castleman killed two, and each of the others one. Naturally, the intrepedity of the act, and the falling of seven of their men so suddenly, confounded the savages; and before they could recover, the whites had retreated and made good their escape into the thick undergrowth. They arrived safely at the station six days afterwards.

On another occasion, Castleman was sent out to search for traces of Indians, as it was rumored that they had threatened another invasion. He took up his route, and going half-bent, his eyes on the alert for traces of the enemy, he reached the war trace perhaps sixty miles from Nashville. This was in 1792. At that distance he discovered traces of a large body of the savages, and hastened home to warn the settlers. The latter fled at once to the stations for protection. In addition to what he had seen on the war trace, he discovered that the camp of Black Fox, which had for some time been on the site of Murfreesboro, was deserted, and construed this to be an indication of danger.

When Castleman returned, to be doubly sure four other scouts—Clayton, Gee, Rains and Kennedy—were sent out to spy. The first two never returned, having been killed, though it was thought that they had gone only farther away than Rains and Kennedy. The latter came in by Buchanan's station, reporting there that there were no Indian signs to be found. The people upon this information felt relieved and began returning to their homes.

Buchanan's station was defended by only about fifteen gun-men. Guards had been put out, as there was still some uneasiness. At midnight on September 30—only a few hours after the report of Rains and Kennedy—there was an alarm given that the Indians were about to attack the fort, their approach being suspected by the running of frightened cattle. So stealthily had they approached, that they were not discovered until within ten paces of the palisades! John McRory, the sentry, fired at them, when the Indians began pouring volley after volley into the log walls. Others attempted to set fire to the buildings. One of them climbed to the roof with a torch, but was shot. Falling to the ground, he continued his efforts to fire the station, when another shot killed him.

It was seen that the attacking party was unusually large from the reports of their guns, and very few persons in the station thought escape from massacre possible. After an hour or so, the Indians retired. It was afterwards learned thaht there were seven hundred warriors present, under the leadership of John Watts —four or five hundred Creeks, two hundred Cherokees, and thirty or forty Shawnees. Next morning it was found that three Indians had been killed, and later, that seven others had been wounded—John Watts, shot in both thighs, White-Man Killer, Dragging Canoe's brother, Owl's son, a young buck from Lookout Mountain and two others from Running Water and the Creek nation. Out on the ground near the fort were picked up a number of pipes, swords, hatchets, and budgets of Indian articles, as well as a handkerchief and moccasin belonging to Gee and Clayton, which were evidence that those scouts had been killed and their belongings taken.

The savages left the community without making another attack. Some years later the Indians explained that they were surprised at the resistance made, and supposed that their attack was expected and that soldiers were still organized ready to defend the settlements.

It is presumed that Castleman's judgment was generally received as good after this affair.

Knoxville is one of the most flourishing cities of Tennessee, and has long been interesting from the standpoint of history. Situated on the Tennessee river, covering what were once wooded hills and valleys that made ideal hiding-places for savage people, and containing half a hundred bridges, it is also one of the most picturesque places in America. In its limits, on one of the neglected streets, stands the ancient capitol of the State; in the beautiful court-house park, and facing Gay street, is the monument to John Sevier, glimmering in the first rays of the rising sun and bathed in its wine-like glow in the evening; near the corner of two streets that are now rarely disturbed by the din of the business portion of town, are the graves of William Blount and his wife; and in the suburbs, on a hill-slope whose peace is intensified in summer by the tinkling of cow bells and made more solemn in winter by the dirgeful winds, may be seen the plain

KNOXVILLE FOUNDED.

two-room cottage which was the early home of America's most celebrated female novelist, Frances Hodgson Burnett. The founder of this city was James White. He was a soldier of the revolutionary war, a member of the House of Representatives of the territory, and speaker of the senate after the territory became a State. This was about the extent of his public service. In 1792 White's small but prosperous settlement invited the location of the seat of the Territorial government, and he laid off the town in sixty-four lots and named the place for Major-General Henry Knox, Secretary of War under Washington. Governor Blount's first abode there after his appointment was in a log cabin situated on a knoll between the present university and the river. As it was the seat of government, and considered generally well guarded, the Indians did not often venture to attack Knoxville, though their depredations were carried on near by for some years after it was founded. But in 1793 a body of a thousand Cherokees and Creeks decided to attack and plunder the town. While the attack was not made, owing to the fact that the principal chiefs, John Watts and Double Head, learned that their plans were probably suspected by the citizens, and anticipating a strong defense, the Knoxvillians conceived one of the most desperate schemes to prevent the fall of the place. They numbered only about forty fighting men, among them being White. They decided to repair to a point out from the fort, where the Indians would probably appear; wait until the enemy were in gunshot range, then fire with as careful precision as possible, and flee to the station to make a final stand. The Indians, having marched in the direction of Clinch river after massacreing the inmates of Cavet's station and giving over the idea of making an assault on Knoxville, the whites were not allowed an opportunity to make a practical test of their heroism; but their determination was a splendid example of the courage of the frontiersmen, the eulogy of which does not become stale and unprofitable no matter how often indulged in.

Andrew Jackson, though he afterwards became one of the most conspicuous characters in American history, did not come prominently into notice until after the most trying days of the pioneers. He had been appointed public prosecutor for the Western District of North Carolina, and arrived in Nashville in 1788. During the first seven years following his arrival, he traveled from Nashville to Jonesborough—a distance of two hundred and eighty miles—twenty-two times in the discharge of his official duties. In 1791 occurred the romance with which his name is connected whenever it is mentioned—his marriage to Mrs. Rachel Robards. She was a daughter of Col. John Donelson, one of the earliest settlers of the Cumberland region, and was first married to Lewis Robards, of Kentucky. This union proved unhappy, and Robards, in the winter of 1790-91, applied to the Legislature of Virginia for a divorce. On the news reaching Nashville that the divorce had been granted, Mrs. Robards and Jackson were married at Natchez. It was afterwards learned, however, that the couple had not been divorced until some months later, and then by judicial action in Kentucky. Jackson and the lady were remarried. While the slowness with which news was passed from settlement to settlement in those days, not to mention the uncertainty of its transmission, thus placed Jackson and his wife in an awkward position, the mistake was sensibly condoned by the public. But Jackson had made enemies, political and private, and they harped on the unfortunate circumstance to injure him. There are few instances on record of a more devoted love of woman than that of Jackson for his wife, and the fact tends to soften the judgment of those who have no admiration for the austere man. But his love embittered at the time it blessed his life, the taunts of his enemies involving him in duels and rancorous discussions. He brooked no unkind reference to his wife, and his life was often risked in defense of her good name. While he was elected to Congress in 1796, and had served the country in other capacities before the end of the eighteenth century, it was after the times with which these stories have to do that his most important distinction was achieved.

CHAPTER XI.

ENDURANCE AND HEROISM OF FRONTIER WOMEN, AND SOME INSTANCES PARTICULARIZED.

The fact that the wives, mothers, daughters and relatives of the pioneers accompanied the latter into the Tennessee wilderness is enough to cause us to regard them as heroines. Many of the women, however, were forced to face conditions which called forth physical prowess and courage that were remarkable. Not a few were carried into captivity, too, and kept in a bondage worse than death by the tomahawk would have been.

Mrs. William Bean occupies a unique place in local history. But few lines are devoted to her family, though Captain William Bean was one of the first settlers of the State, and their son, Russell, was the first white child born in Tennessee. It has been a long time since Bean brought his dutiful wife from Pittslyvania County, Virginia, and built a cabin by the Watauga; and, yet, when we consider the incident which left him for awhile desolate, a touch of the sadness which was his, and which lingers like an echo among the hills, is transferred through the vicissitudes of the years to affect the sympathetic reader of to-day.

She may have been fair enough, this Virginia matron, to have inspired the poet's cadenced compliment; a descendant, doubtless, of English ancestors, with graceful step, and of whom it might be said, "One looked her happy eyes within, and heard the nightingales." Forsaking all others, she came with her husband to the wilderness—doubting the wisdom of the movement, perhaps, but duplicating in her submission to him the constancy of Ruth.

When their child was born, the wilderness became less a wilderness. Their cabin was a rude affair, but the little one transfigured the surroundings. The tender greeting of their parents were not heard in the new home, but the prattle of the baby was sweet; and no music the husband ever heard could compare with the mother's voice as she sang it to sleep. Seven years went by. Other families came and found homes in the neighborhood, until somewhat of the old social pleasures of the communities they had forsaken were secured. A fort had been built, and the cabins and fields were more numerous and extended. The pigs rummaging among the leaves for mast. the cows lowing at the lot bars, the cackle of the chickens out in the fields, and the song of the laborer following his rude plow through the furrows, gave the neighborhood a homelike appearance, and denoted thrift. But all these things did not escape the Indians' notice. They incited their jealousy and fear. and—instigated by the agents of the cause of England, for the revolution had commenced—they invaded the settlement in 1776, and

Mrs. Bean was captured by them and carried into captivity. There is no record of the husband's efforts to recapture her, but of course these were not lacking. After she was taken into captivity Mrs. Bean was condemned to death. She was bound, taken to the top of one of the mounds, and was about to be burned, when Nancy Ward, an Indian woman, liberated her and had her restored to her friends.

This was only one of the many acts of Nancy Ward showing her friendliness to the whites, and she merits our gratitude. In behalf of mercy, she often felt justified in betraying the contemplated attacks of her people on the settlements. She was an Indian prophetess, and a niece of the reigning vice-king, Atta-Kulla-Kulla, of the Cherokee nation. Her father was a British officer. She was born about 1740. James Robertson visited her in 1772, and described her as a woman "queenly and commanding," and her lodge furnished in a style of barbaric splendor. She must have possessed remarkable traits to have wielded autocratic influence over the Cherokees when they knew she was friendly to the whites. Even the king, Oconostota, had to give way to her in peace or war, and her sway was evidenced in the case of Mrs. Bean.

About four years after Mrs. Bean's release, another female was captured, this time from the section of the Cumberland country called Neelly's Bend. This was a daughter of Captain Neelly. He was one of the earliest settlers there, and as Indians had not for some time been seen in the neighborhood, he resolved to camp in the bend and experiment in making salt. He was assisted by several of the whites of Mansker's, not far from the station, and had one of his daughters to accompany him to perform the duties of cooking for the men who were cutting wood, filling the kettle with sulphur water, and keeping up fires. Neelly hunted buffalo and deer to feed the hands. One day, being much fatigued after a long hunt, he returned to the camp, threw down his deer, and lay down to rest. His daughter skinned one of the venison hams and prepared it for supper. The dogs had gone with the laborers, and Neelly was soon asleep. Passing in and out of the tent, unconscious of danger, she was startled to hear the firing of guns near by. Her father raised himself half up, then fell back dead. Indians entered the camp, and after seizing her father's gun and powder horn, took her captive. The murderers apparently thought they would be pursued, and did not tarry at the camp any longer than it took them to gather the few articles they deemed of use. An Indian held her by either arm and compelled her to run. They traveled all night, and the girl was finally carried to the Creek Nation. It is pleasant to transcribe the assurance of Putnam that "after several years' captivity she was released—exchanged, married reputably in Kentucky, and made a good and exemplary wife and Christian mother."

Sometime before 1795 the home of Colonel Tilsworth, also of the Cumberland settlements, was attacked in his absence, and all of his family killed except his daughter. In the summer of 1795 he heard that the Creeks who had taken his daughter captive were desirous of exchanging prisoners; and receiving a passport went in search of her. The information received from him on his return gave an idea of how captives were treated.

His daughter was not carried at once to the nation, but the savages retained her in the woods at their camp on the Tennessee river for months, finally carrying her into the nation. The Spanish agent there had offered her captors four hundred dollars for her, desiring to send her to school at New Orleans. At the camp on the Tennessee she was compelled to cut wood, make fires, and bring water; and upon her arrival in the nation she pounded corn and made meal, and was whipped and in other respects treated as a slave.

These are only a few recorded cases out of many. Haywood occasionally refers to this state of affairs. One of his rambling paragraphs is that in 1793 "many of our people were in slavery with the Creek Indians, and were treated by them in all respects as slaves." In the Cavelegies, Mrs. Williams and child; Alice Thompson, of Nashville; Mrs. Caffrey and child, of Nashville. In the Hog villages, Mr. Brown, of the district of Mero; in the Clewatly town, Miss Scarlet; in the White Grounds, Miss Wilson, of the district of Mero, and a boy and girl; in the Colummies, a boy of five years of age; at the Big Talassee, a boy eight or ten years of age, and a girl seven or eight years of age; in the Pocontala-hasse, a boy twelve or thirteen years of age; in the Oakfuskee, a lad fifteen years of age; in the Red Ground, a man called John; in Casauders, a boy whose age and name were not known; in Lesley Town, a young woman who was repeatedly threatened with death for refusing to look with favor on Lesley's son; and in some other town were Mrs. Crocket and her son. The list of women and children taken into captivity from the earliest settlement to 1800 would number hundreds. The fate of the captives was sad indeed; women were forced often to become the wives of the savages who had slain their relatives; brothers and sisters were separated until they lost all knowledge of each other. Some were exchanged after months or years, while others never saw their friends again. It may be well enough for our peace of mind that we know so little of the captives and their lives, of their heartaches and physical sufferings.

Of scores of instances of the heroism of the women of the settlements, only a few have been preserved. The case of Mrs. Buchanan, when seven hundred savages attacked Buchanan's station, near Nashville, in 1792, is a notable one. On that occasion, when there were only fifteen men to defend the station, she fired repeatedly at the enemy, and had other women to mould bullets or make a display of men's hats to deceive the Indians as to the number of men present. She afterwards said she had killed buffalo and deer, and if her aim had been as true as she endeavored to make it, some Indian must have suffered from the gun in her hand at the time of the attack.

Houston's station was erected in East Tennessee, about six miles from the little town of Maryville, and was occupied by the families of Houston, McConnell, McEwen, Sloane and Henry. In 1785 it was attacked by a party of Indians one hundred strong. They had been robbing and murdering, and were elated over their success. They made a vigorous assault, having no doubt about reducing the fort. But some of the best riflemen on the frontiers were in this station, and they were greatly aided by the women. The efforts of Mrs. McEwen were especially praiseworthy. As the gallant defenders loaded and discharged their guns with rapidity she melted lead and run the bullets for the gun-men, keeping them fully supplied. A bullet from without passed between the logs at one time, going close to her, and, striking the wall, rolled upon the floor at her feet. Picking it up instantly, she carried it to her husband, with the cool request, "Here is a ball run out of the Indians' lead; send it back to them as quick as possible."

In 1787 Captain Gillespie lived in his cabin on the French Broad, twelve miles from Dumplin station. His family consisted of himself, his wife and a child. One morning he left home for Dumplin, not suspecting that the Indians were in the neighborhood. The day before he had been burning brush on a little clearing, and, as fortune would have it, the smoke was still rising the morning he left home, in plain view of the house. A small band of savages came by, and, finding Mrs. Gillespie unprotected, entered the house. They might not have intended committing murder; probably they thought only of plunder and annoying Mrs. Gillespie; but the settlers had learned to expect no mercy from the red men.

One of the intruders—a burly, ferocious fellow—took out his scalping knife and drew it across his bare arm as if to whet it. Then, approaching the cradle where the infant was slumbering, he indicated with his finger a line around its head, as if having an intention to scalp it. Another Indian who had entered stood looking on, his grim features showing that he was enjoying the mother's agony immensely.

For a moment she stood as though paralyzed; then springing to the door and looking towards the clearing, called out:

"White men, come home! Indians! Indians!"

The warriors were disconcerted by the stratagem, dashed from the cabin toward the spring and disappeared in the cane. Mrs. Gillespie took her babe in her arms, left the house and fled in the direction of Dumplin. She was not followed, and after going several miles met her husband on his return.

On the night of May 25, 1795, George Mann, who lived above Knoxville, heard a noise at his stable, and left his house to ascertain the cause. Discovering nothing unusual, he started to return, when he was intercepted by Indians and wounded. Fleeing to a cave a short distance off, he was dragged forth and killed.

Mrs. Mann had heard the report of the guns, and the footfalls of the savages pursuing her husband. Listening intently, she soon heard the tramp of feet approaching and the low words of the Indians, who seemed to be unusually careless of the noise they were making, thinking, perhaps, that there were none to fear in the house.

The rifle was taken from its rack, and, leveling it at a crevice near the door, Mrs. Mann awaited the slayers of her husband. A savage pushed open the door. She could see in the uncertain light that he was followed by others. The children, as yet, had not been awakened. Pulling the trigger of the gun held steadily in her hands, she fired, and the foremost Indian fell in the doorway. There was a scream from the one just behind, and it was evident that two had been hit by her unerring aim. This warm reception caused the Indians to gather up their wounded and leave the house. She had not screamed or uttered a word, and the perfect silence must have impressed the attacking party with the supposition that there were armed men within. Before leaving the place, however, they burned the barn and outbuildings.

"Granny" Hays lived near Donelson's station, east of Nashville. She was an elderly woman, and was one female who never appeared frightened when the savages were around. She was devoid of fear. She lived in a small cabin alone, but sometimes had as a sort of charity-guest a lame, half-witted young fellow named Tim Dunbar. One day he was out in the garden, when some Indians fired at him. He ran into the house, exclaiming that he was killed, leaving the gate and door open. "You fool! you are not hurt," cried Granny Hays. "Get up and take your gun and follow me. Be quick, before they have time to reload their guns."

Making the frightened dolt follow, she went out to the gate and literally "shelled the bushes," where the Indians had been seen; then re-entering the cabin and barring the door, they reloaded and awaited a near approach of the savages. The latter kept out of range, firing occasionally at the house.

Some one saw the fire of Donelson's station, which was destroyed on this invasion of the Indians, and had men from Caffrey's fort, near the mouth of Stone's river, to hasten to the relief of the old lady. It required considerable pursuasion to get her to go to a more secure place.

CHAPTER XII.

THE PASTIMES OF THE SETTLERS, AND THEIR WHOLE-SOULED HOSPITALITY.

Despite the dangers surrounding them, and the innumerable hardships embarrassing everywhere, the settlers managed to get not a little enjoyment out of existence. There were clouds in their skies, but there were also sunbeams to break through. They cultivated a spirit of extracting pleasure from the turmoil, in obedience to a demand of nature for some relaxation. And after all, does not enjoyment lie much in the will? If there are those who, though having ears and eyes, refuse to hear and see, to paraphrase Scripture, cannot the reverse be true also?

"By looking, we may see the rose; and, listening, hear a song."

The chase and hunt have afforded pleasure since the days of Nimrod, the majority of men not being actuated by the thoughts of the versatile Louise Imogen Guiney to the effect that "our father Adam is said to have dwelt in peace with all the beasts in his garden. And there is no evidence in the Mosaic annals that it was they who became perverted, and broke faith with

OLD-TIME COOKING.

man. Marry, man himself, in the birth of his moral ugliness, set up the hateful division, estranged these estimable friends, and then, unto everlasting, pursues, maligns, subjugates, and kills the beings braver, shrewder and more innocent than he." The hunt and chase were open to the settlers. Where we grow enthusiastic in hunting small game, they could enjoy the bringing in of deer, bear and buffalo, not to mention the wolves and panthers that were as plentiful as squirrels. If there was a log-rolling or house-raising or wedding, one could step out and in a few hours return with a deer or half-dozen turkeys for the occasion. Flocks of a hundred turkeys would sometimes be seen within a few yards of the cabins. Our foremothers, according to an early and reliable chronicler, could not be excelled in preparing this wild game. "There were no cooks to be named in the same day with them when the cooking of buffalo tongue, bear meat and venison is mentioned," he enthusiastically exclaims. "And the good housewife in those days rightfully gloried in the baking of the hoe-cake, ash-cake, and Johnny cake. Then, after frost, when opossums and persimmons were ripe, and any one mentioned good eating, the universal exclamation was, 'Oh ho; don't talk!'"

There was relief from low spirits in making and baiting wolf-traps, and in building turkey-pens when the game had grown wary, although some of those thus engaged were not infrequently shot and killed by lurking Indians. Bears and wolves for years after the first settlement of Middle Tennessee were found in great numbers, especially in the Harpeth hills, ten or twelve miles from Nashville. The bear hunt was laborious and dangerous, but hunters and their dogs were very partial to it.

There were parties in which the young people, without reference to previous standing in the social circles they had gone in in Virginia, the Carolinas and the older colonies, found much recreation and real enjoyment. What mattered the seamy floors and bear-oil lights, the uncouth costumes and the scant furniture? There were fiddling and dancing and refreshments at these functions, and good will and jollity prevailed. "Never were the story, the joke, the song and the laugh better enjoyed than upon the hewed blocks, or puncheon stools around the roaring log fire of the early Western settler," observes Kendall. "The lyre of Apollo was not hailed with more delight in primitive Greece, than the advent of the first fiddler among the dwellers of the wilderness; and the polished daughters of the East never enjoyed themselves half so well, moving to the music of a full band, upon the elastic floor of their ornamented ball-room, as did the daughters of the emigrants, keeping time to a self-taught fiddler on the bare earth or the puncheon floor of the primitive log cabin."

Shooting-matches, throwing the tomahawk, jumping, boxing and wrestling, as well as foot and horse racing, were also indulged in.

THE SOCIAL VISIT. 133

Perhaps the social visit yielded as much pleasure as any other pastime, for men are pre-eminently social by nature, and in the wilderness the people were much like those at Grigsby's Station—celebrated by James Whitcomb Riley—where every neighbor was dear as a relation, and the latchstring was always hanging from the door!

These visits were doubtless more enjoyable in the evenings, after the day's work was over. Some large family—parents and a train of children of all ages—might be seen to fasten the door and walk down a lonely lane in the direction of a small cabin, whose window, with open shutter and greased paper screen, glowed a blossom of the dark. On the way they might have heard the snarl of a wild animal among the gloomy woods, while nearer an owl would slowly flap by, snapping its beak as it passed over their heads. As they neared their destination, the bay of the house dog rang out, or, what was more probable, the yelp of hounds would sound in a confused chorus, while the head of the house came out and yelled to the canines to be gone.

Arriving, a semi-circle would be drawn about the spacious fire-place, more fuel would be thrown upon the already roaring fire, and a bit more bear's oil added to the rudely improvised lamp. The ruddy blaze would drive the lurking shadows out of the room, or make ludicrous silhouettes on the plain log walls, or light up the old flint-lock rifle resting in a rack above the door. Maybe the hunk of venison or bear meat in the pot hanging in the chimney was getting near enough done for the morrow's meal to be taken from the fire by the garrulous housewife and put on a shelf, while the husband, with growing enthusiasm, explained how the game was taken. The news was touched upon. What was the latest from Washington's army? So Cornwallis had been caught napping, had he? Had Sevier's last raid into the Indian country proved enough to cow the murderous savages? How was the Cumberland settlement progressing? The victory of King's Mountain was due to the courage of Nollichucky Jack and Shelby, was it not? Had no tidings been brought in recently by the scouts relative to Watts' or Hanging Maw's intentions? The Watauga people had proved too much for Old Abraham's and Dragging Canoe's warriors, had they not?

After awhile the gossip of the settlement would be retailed; or at the request of the children, now drawing nearer their elders, stories of adventures would be told, of hairbreadth escapes, of individual instances of valor where Indian or bear or panther was pitted against a white man; or what was not infrequent, a thrilling tale of spooks was narrated, whereat the small listeners would cast furtive glances behind them and edge in between the fire and the old folks.

The coming of emigrants, or their passing through the settlements to some remoter post, was an event of importance and even pleasure; for they brought news from the distant and older spots of civilization, and added strength to the new. On this point Ramsey says: "The new-comer, on his arrival in the settlements was everywhere and at all times greeted with cordial welcome. Was he without a family? He was at once taken in as a cropper or a farming hand, and found a home in the kind family of some settler. Had he a wife and children? They were all asked, in backwoods phrase, 'to camp with us till the neighbors can put up a cabin for you.' The invitation accepted, the family where he stops is duplicated, but this inconvenience is of short duration. The host goes around the neighborhood, mentions the arrival of the strangers, appoints a day, close at hand, for the neighbors to meet and provide them a home. After the cabin is raised and the new-comers are in it, every family, near at hand, bring in something to give them a start. A pair of pigs, a cow and a calf, a pair of all the domestic fowls—any supplies of the necessaries of life which they have—all are brought and presented to the beginners. If they have come into the settlement in the spring, the neighbors make another frolic, and clear and fence a field for them."

No; not entirely without their honest pleasures—including the feeling of joy rising in the reflection that it is more blessed to give than receive—were the foreparents. There was a time to smile as well as to weep; recollections of triumph as well as memories of defeat; instances of Heaven's blessings to bid hope live during the years of disaster and the long-suffering.

CHAPTER XIII.

EARLY RELIGIOUS SENTIMENT, AND THE FAITHFUL WORK OF THE MINISTERS.

Bishop Asbury, who was greatly interested in the spiritual welfare of the pioneers, wrote in his diary in 1797: "When I reflect that not one in a hundred came here to get religion, but rather to get plenty of good land, I think it will be well if some or many do not lose their souls."

The prevalent evil which the ministers refer to as the lust of greed was sufficient to make one think of the Scriptural averment that we cannot serve both God and mammon. Yet there is little doubt that under their affliction the settlers were more prone to yearn, in the words of Mrs. Ward, to feel themselves in some grasp that sustained, some hold that made life more tolerable again. Instinctively, it might be said—even if there had not been that deep religious fervor which had for some years pervaded the communities from which they emigrated—the people as a general thing meditated on the Creator and found comfort in His promises. Putnam records the fact that the women, especially, of the Cumberland country were well educated in the doctrines of revealed religion; they brought

THE CAMP-MEETING. 137

their Bibles with them, and offered the first prayers in the wilderness. There were also many pious women and men in the eastern settlements.

But a time came early in their history when all lukewarmness, all torpor, would give way to a wave of religious zeal scarcely equaled since the days of Pentecost. The great revival of 1800, which may be considered an epoch in the affairs of the Southwest, was nearing.

It is not overstepping the truth of history to say that the camp-meeting was one of the greatest factors in forwarding the civilization and moral development of the West, especially of Tennessee and Kentucky, and impressing reverence for institutions having their origin in the divine fiat; that have withstood the assaults of the iconoclast, the sneers of the irreverent, and the encroachments of the foreign element seeking to discard some of the wisest and holiest boons proffered mankind. To them as well as the ministers who faced death and every manner of hardship for the pioneers, is due the reverence with which we hold the Sabbath with its "silent theater, the houses from which the sounds of music are banished, the empty streets, the calm stillness of the day"—our Sunday, which the laborer will do well to hold against the insidious efforts of trade and commerce if he values the rest which God knew in the beginning his nature would require!

One hundred and thirty-eight heads of Tennessee families had united in calling Rev. Charles Cummings to come and settle among them as pastor, and he ministered to the people thirty-nine years. He was a Presbyterian, and was the first man who ever preached in Tennessee. He often carried his rifle to church with him, seeing that it was well-primed as he set it down conveniently near the pulpit before announcing his text. "His first years in this wild frontier," says McDonnold in his history of Cumberland Presbyterianism in the West, "were tracked with the blood of Indian battles. He fought often, and had many narrow escapes."

The country called Cumberland lay partly in Tennessee and partly in Kentucky, its southern boundary being the dividing ridge between Cumberland and Duck rivers in Tennessee, and its northern boundary Green river in Kentucky. Another Presbyterian, Thomas B. Craighead, was the first pastor who settled in this section. He was followed by Rev. Benjamin Ogden, of the Methodist Church. One of Craighead's sayings, according to McDonnold. was: "I would not give this old handkerchief for all the experimental religion in the world."

But the departure of Rev. James McGready, who would now be called an evangelist, and the arrival of the Methodists, brought about the camp-meetings and finally the great religious revival, wherein experimental religion was given much weight.

McDonnold says that it is strange that mere conjectural accounts of the origin of camp-meetings should be exclusively published, when we have the most reliable accounts from eye-witnesses. He avers that the first camp-meeting in Christendom, that was appointed and intended for a camp-meeting, was at Gaspar River church, in Kentucky. After this, camp-meetings became the order of the day.

The early camp-meetings were without tents or other shelter except the wagons. Later, people built double log cabins, which were still called tents, for their families and visitors. So far as possible people cooked the provisions before they left home, and they moved to camp expecting to remain during the meeting. All who attended were fed freely. Campers would go out into the crowd and make a public invitation for all to come and eat. The camps were supplied with straw, both on the ground and on the bed scaffolds. One tent was used by the ladies, and another by the gentlemen. A field of grain with water running through it was secured, and the horses of the visitors turned into it. A vast shelter covered with boards was built and seated for a preaching place. This also had straw for a floor. In the intervals between public services it was the usual custom to go alone, or in small groups to secret prayer in an adjacent forest. Gentlemen were not allowed to go upon the ladies' grounds. And in all the early days, before railroads came along, these meetings were not only as orderly as any other kind of meetings, but they were generally seasons of unparalleled solemnity and unequaled moral grandeur.

At these revivals, the attendance was large, the interest intense. People came for miles to different camp-grounds in Tennessee, and remained for days. "A peculiar physical manifestation accompanied these revivals, popularly known as the jerks," observes Phelan. "They were involuntary and irresistible. When under their influence, the sufferers would dance, or sing, or shout. Sometimes they would sway from side to side, or throw the head backwards and forwards, or leap, or spring. Generally those under the influence would at the end fall upon the ground and remain rigid for hours, and sometimes whole multitudes would become dumb and fall prostrate. As the swoon passed away, the sufferer would weep piteously, moan, and sob. After a while the gloom would lift, a smile of heavenly peace would radiate the countenance, and words of joy and rapture would break forth, and conversion always followed. Even the most skeptical, even the scoffers, who visited these meetings for the purpose of showing their hardihood would be taken in this way."

This wave of religion, called the great revival, beginning in 1797 under James McGready, rescued Kentucky and Tennessee, and through them the West and South, from French infidelity.

The recollections of John Carr are interesting and valuable. He was a pioneer and historian, and lived during the times he has described, being one of the settlers on the Cumberland when the attack was in 1792 made on Buchanan's Station by John Watts and others. The ministers wore no beards in those days, according to Carr. "I have little doubt,*"* he says, "had they risen in the pulpit in that manner (with beards), most of the congregation would have left the house." There was much prejudice against jewelry. The people were ignorant of the early Methodist class-meetings. An itinerant held services at the cabin of Carr's parents, closing with a class-meeting, in which the people were each questioned relative to spiritual matters. The preacher had drawn a bench across the door, and was proceeding with his examination, when he drew near Thomas Hamilton, who had fought during the revolutionary war, and was one of the bravest men in the settlement. Hamilton grew nervous, looked anxiously toward the back of the house, where his hat was, and then in the direction of the chimney. He finally sprang to his feet, climbed out the chimney, mounted his horse and rode to his home five miles distant, a thoroughly scared man.

On another occasion there was to be a ball in the settlements. It was well advertised, and the young people looked forward to it with pleasure. Rev. James O'Cull was in the neighborhood, heard of the contemplated ball, and managed to arrive at the house where it was to take place and at the proper date. He asked permission of his host to preach, and turned the ball into a revival.

Among the earlier ministers who came to Tennessee besides Bishop Asbury, Craighead, Cummings and

Ogden, were Samuel Doak, Learner Blackman, Barnabas McHenry, Peter Massie, Hezekiah Balch, Samuel Carrick, James Shaw and James Balch. Their labors were ceaseless, and the fruits of their exertions correspondingly good. Gilmore insists that the majority of the first settlers were "hardshell" Baptists; but the advent of the Presbyterian and Methodist ministers soon changed this condition, if it really existed.

Few more picturesque figures than that of the frontier preacher show through the haze of the years. Very plainly dressed, but having due regard for cleanliness; open and frank of countenance, with a strength and kindness blended in his face, strange to see in a person of his unaffected manner—but really not so hard to account for when we reflect that while he toiled through the jostlings of existence, his thoughts had communion daily and hourly with the Creator. As he came and went, he had a smile for the children, and no man could point through long years of service and self-denial to one word of his that purposely left a sting, to one act that would lead men to think he was not fit to step up from earth into the presence of Deity. A little impractical, maybe, in business affairs, and pinched sometimes for the necessaries of life; but, as has been beautifully said by Dr. Watson, of Weelum Maclure, it was all for mercy's sake. For his mind was turned toward saving souls, and not on business; his labor was given to his Maker, and men did not then pay as though they realized that he was one of those of whom the world was not worthy. As he passed from station to station, the wilderness seemed to become brighter; and as he knelt in the humble homes of the poor and prayed in the sincerity of his soul, there came back to earth some semblance of Eden out where the cattle strayed on the hills, where the birds twittered in the canes, where the runnel flowed murmuringly to the river like a happy child-soul journeying from the dawn of life to the twilight of eternity, and where the few old-fashioned roses in the little yards leaned in the breeze that hurried through the vales and over the hills to caress them with invisible but woman-soft hands. Giving each person a cordial handshake, smiling sunlight into the hearts of the children, dispensing in his humble way the bread of life—"the spiritually indispensable," as Carlyle has it—visiting the sick and pointing the faltering soul heavenward that it might lean on the Everlasting arms, he appears one of the noblest works of God.

CHAPTER XIV.

THE TRIBES CLAIMING A RIGHT TO LANDS AT THE FIRST SETTLEMENT, AND THEIR PRESENT STATUS.

Like truth, reason, when crushed to earth, will rise again; and if selfishness or ire has been too strong for our nobler instincts, reason will reproach us with the fact when calmness returns. Since the last tribe of Indians gave up all interest in Tennessee soil and sought other hunting grounds, we have had time to reflect. The present generation's prejudices are not awakened by the personal recollection of Indian butcheries, and the coolness required for the dealing out of justice exists. Was the treatment which the savages received always what it should have been? Cannot instances of dishonest dealings and inhumanity on the part of the whites be pointed out? The earlier pioneers of America in some cases sowed the wind in broken promises and injustices; and the generation of pioneers coming after them reaped the whirlwind of savage hate and resentment. "And the barbarous people showed us no little kindness, for they kindled a fire, and received us every one, because of the present rain, and because of the cold," writes Paul of his experiences on the island of Melita. Those who came from Europe to the New World were generally met as kindly by the Indians; and yet the latter learned that selfishness and duplicity were common to the advance guard of American civilization.

To the lover of liberty thoughts of the partition of Poland arouse the resentment as of a personal wrong; but sadder than this is the driving of a people, however necessary for progress, from their country. Though the Indians have had no historian to present their side of the controversy or herald their best deeds, the world will admit that their more than half of a century's war against the whites was sublime in its desperation and determined courage. The most enthusiastic adherent of the great mission of the Anglo-Saxon people must see something pathetic in the efforts of the Indians, who saw treaties disregarded, and continuous encroachments made on domains claimed by them; who yet were not deterred from going to war for their rights though they knew that defeat and probably extinction would be the result.

The origin of the American Indians has been a matter for debate for centuries. While their language fails to connect them with any Asiatic families, their modes of life and implements are thought to connect them with the earlier races of the Eastern continent whose relics are found in mounds and shell heaps. And this is about all that has been proven after centuries of investigation and theorizing.

At the period of the first exploration of Tennessee, vague and indefinite claims to certain portions of the country were made by a number of Indian tribes, but none of it was held by permanent occupancy, "except," as Ramsey explains, "that section embraced by the segment of a circle, of which the Tennessee river is the periphery, from the point where it intersects the North Carolina line to that where this stream enters the State of Alabama." The Cherokees were settled there. The Shawnees, Chickasaws, Choctaws and Cherokees claimed other portions, their lines being merely ideal ones.

The Shawnees, according to the early French explorers, were said to assert a right to the lower Cumberland; but they were even then a wandering people. The Indians informed Gen. James Robertson on one occasion that about 1665 the Shawnees occupied the country from the Tennessee river to where Nashville stands, and north of the Cumberland, but that about 1700 they emigrated north and were received as a wandering tribe by the Six Nations. Another account was given by a Cherokee chief, Little Corn Planter, in 1772. He said that the Shawnees removed a hundred years before from the Savannah river to the Cumberland by permission of his people, but about 1700 the Cherokees, assisted by the Chickasaws, drove them from the Cumberland valley. About 1714, when M. Charleville opened a store on the site of Nashville, he is said to have occupied their old fort. The fact that there were no Indians around Nashville when the first settlers came is accounted for on the theory that the tribes had been trying to destroy each other and, becoming afraid to meet, abandoned the country. Evidences were very numerous that a dense population had once occupied the section said to have been the home of the Shawnees. When the first settlers arrived on the Cumberland, they found by every lasting spring collections of graves, "made in a particular way," explains Haywood, "with the heads inclined on the sides and feet stones, the whole covered with a stratum of mold and dirt about eight or ten inches deep." In addition to these was the appearance of walls inclosing ancient habitations. A part of the bandits infesting the narrows of the Tennessee, making war on emigrants and navigators, were Shawnees.

The Chickasaws laid claim to all the territory in Kentucky and Tennessee lying between the Tennessee and Mississippi rivers, and a portion north of the former, though they had no settlements in those sections. In 1735 their warriors were estimated at hardly five hundred; but they were war-like, and generally friendly to the whites. Piomingo, a chief, was a staunch and trusted friend of the early settlers. The Choctaws and Chickasaws are believed to have had a common origin, as their appearance, laws and traditions are similar.

The Cherokees were perhaps the most powerful Indian nation in the South. It is said that at one time they had sixty-four populous towns, and their warriors were estimated at above six thousand. They were continually at war, however—the over-hill towns with the northern towns, and the lower ones with the Creeks—and became considerably diminished before the settlements were begun on Watauga. Later, the frontiers of Georgia, Virginia, and North and South Carolina were greatly distressed by them. Their native land lay upon the Catawba, the Yadkin, Keowee, Tugaloo, Flint, Coosa, Etowah, on the east and south, and on a number of the tributaries of the Tennessee on the west and north. They were a mountain people, and loved their country as the traditional William Tell loved his. War was a passion with them; but, when they took to the arts of peace, they made the most rapid strides in civilization. They claimed that they dispossessed a moon-eyed people, unable to see by day.

The Muskogee or Creek Indians were inveterate enemies of the first settlers of the State, though they had no settlements within its boundaries, and were therefore actuated mainly by a desire to plunder or by hatred of the white race.

There were quite a number of savage chiefs who were justly celebrated for gifts that would have elevated them to high places if they had been identified with civilized communities. Foresight, diplomacy, oratory, military genius, all these had brilliant representation even as late as the eighteenth century.

Oconostota was an orator as well as a warrior, and was head king of the Cherokees. Nothing is known of his birth, but he had attained the age of manhood in

A Cherokee King.

1730, and was living as late as 1809, being referred to in a letter of that date from Return J. Meigs, Indian agent, as "greasy old Oconostota" who would intrude on his studies and wail for hours over his departed greatness. He was, in his prime, of herculean frame, undaunted courage, and great physical prowess. He was one of the six delegates who, in 1730, visited George II. in England, being eight years later elected head king of the Cherokees. He exerted despotic sway not only over his own people but over the Creeks.

He opposed the treaty of 1775, whereby much of the territory of the Indians was ceded, and made an eloquent speech. Over-ruled, he signed the treaty, but said to Daniel Boone: "Young man, we have sold you a fine territory, but I fear you will have some difficulty in getting it settled." For years he made war on the whites, carrying out this implied threat.

Finally, his nation dethroned him, and he became an inebriate. For nearly thirty years he is known to have wandered about a homeless, weak, besotted and despised man, begging provisions and drink, though claiming Chota, the Cherokee city of refuge, as his home.

The vice king, Atta-Kulla-Kulla, or the Little Carpenter, was for a long time after the erection of Fort Loudoun a friend of the English. He possessed many fine traits. At the time of the butchery of the chiefs left as hostages in Fort Prince George, as narrated in another chapter, a number of whites were still in the Indian towns, and would have been immediately slain if not tortured to death, had he not concealed them until there was an opportunity to escape. He then urged relentless war on the settlements. After the massacre at the Katy Harlin Reserve, he saved the life of an old friend, Capt. Stuart, who was held by Oconostota for the purpose of managing the cannon taken at Fort Loudoun and training them on the defenses of the whites. When the Cherokees were beaten, he was instrumental in bringing about the peace treaty. He lived to a ripe age.

Piomingo, or Mountain Leader, was a leading Chickasaw chief. He was during his last years one of the few faithful friends the whites had among the Indians.

John Watts, a Cherokee, was prominent in the various onslaughts on the settlements. He was one of the most treacherous of his race. While enjoying a wide influence among his people, succeeding in raising large numbers for plunder and revenge, his success for some reason was limited. In none of his actions did anything occur to draw to him the idea of "noble" as Cooper applied it to the red man.

Perhaps Alexander McGillivray, a Creek, was the greatest of the Southern Indians of the last half of the eighteenth century. He was a half-breed, educated at Charleston, South Carolina. During the struggles of the Eastern and Western settlers of Tennessee, he was generally their enemy, and a friend of Spain. He had considerable influence among all the tribes, and from 1784 to his death in 1793, one of his hopes was

MIGRATION BEGUN.   151

to destroy the Cumberland community. He was winning in his manner, but deceitful in his friendships; wealthy, but clung to the squalid life of his people. Lacking the idea of moral rectitude, he was yet now and then known to display surprising generosity, as in the ransoming of white prisoners and restoring them to their friends. He died at Pensacola in 1793.

As pathetic as their contest with the whites was the Indians' final submission to the inevitable—to become exiles from the scenes they had learned to love and the graves which held the bones of their dead. Soon after the fall of Etowah and Nickojack, no doubt there began to be cherished a very strong desire to emigrate to other wilds; and as early as 1790 a few hunters left and went beyond the Mississippi river. In their desire to migrate, they were encouraged by the government which had men like James Robertson, Silas Dinsmore and Return J. Meigs at the various agencies to give flattering suggestions as to the region beyond the Mississippi and to offer to buy the lands claimed by the Indians in Tennessee and on its borders. The extinguishment of their titles appeared to be one of the principle policies of those in power. Threats, flattery, bribery, finesse, and arguments were brought to bear, until at last contracts were concluded, the Indians selling for a mere song. From the tone of "the great argument"—signed July 19, 1798, by James Robertson, James Stuart and Lachlin McIntosh, and addressed to the commissioners of the United States for holding a treaty with the Cherokees—it is reasonable to infer that if the latter had not yielded, force might ultimately have been employed.

Oconostota's prophecy in 1775 that the invader would force the Indian steadily before him across the Mississippi ever towards the West, to find a shelter and a refuge in the seclusion of solitude, was being fulfilled. Those tribes which relinquished their titles to lands and migrated in the first part of the nineteenth century beyond the father of waters, are still being pushed westward. Among the score or so of reservations in the Indian Territory are those of the Shawnees, the Choctaws, the Chickasaws and the Cherokees. The first is in the northeast corner, east of the Neosho; the second in the southeast, bordering Arkansas and Texas; the third joins the Choctaws on the west and is separated from Texas by the Red river; while the fourth lies in the northeast, bordering Kansas and Arkansas. The three last tribes have made considerable strides in agriculture and the mechanics. Taking sides with the Southern Confederacy during the war between the States, they were much weakened, however. Their slaves were freed, and their rights declared forfeited by the United States government. There are many Christians among these Indians, and the missionaries have given them in their language the whole Bible, with spellers, definers, tracts and hymn books.

As the years go by, will the Indians retain, like the Jews, their identity as a people? This is not impossible;

but one of their race, Simon Pokagon, chief of the Pottawattamies, made these observations in a paper in *The Forum* in 1898: "The index-finger of the past and present is pointing to the future, showing most conclusively that by the middle of the twentieth century all Indian reservations and tribe relations will have passed away. Then our people will begin to scatter; and the result will be a general mixing up of the races. Through intermarriage the blood of our people, like the waters that flow into the great ocean, will be forever lost in the dominant race; and generations yet unborn will read in history of the red men of the forest, and inquire, 'Where are they?'"

It is said that a number of the tribes occupying the Indian Territory in 1899 have long contemplated going to Mexico, where they hope for immunity from the whites who are still intruding upon them, and proving the truth of the remark of a statesman that the white race has never shown that charity for the weaker which we should expect from its creeds.

CHAPTER XV.

THE MOUND BUILDERS OR STONE GRAVE RACE, AND SOME ARCHÆOLOGICAL RESEARCHES.

Throughout Tennessee are to be found stone graves, mounds and ruins of forts which tell of a race of people more civilized than the tribes with which the settlers came in contact in the eighteenth century. They are scattered in the valleys of East Tennessee and the lower valley of the Cumberland, but the most populous centers seem to have been in the vicinity of Nashville. The race leaving those ruins is called the Mound Builders or Stone Grave race. Thruston, in his excellent work on the antiquities of Tennessee, observes that it is difficult to ascertain the exact relation of the race and its near kindred of the neighboring States to the historic red Indian, but in the scale of civilization it should probably be classed with the best types of the sedentary or village Indians of New Mexico or Arizona. "If we could have been given a glimpse of the fair valley of the Cumberland in 1492, the date of the Columbian discovery," says he, "it is quite probable that we should have found some of these ancient settlements full of busy life. We might have learned the story of the mounds and graves from some of their

Conflicting Theories. 155

own builders; but nearly three centuries elapsed before the pioneers of civilization reached the confines of Tennessee."

At the period of early European settlement upon the Atlantic coast, and for more than a century later, the French discoverers show that the Indian occupants of the interior section of America were involved in constant warfare with each other, as recorded. Were the Mound Builders on the Cumberland and in various parts of Tennessee overwhelmed and driven off by more savage conquerors, or did they become members of the Shawnee or the Natchez tribe? It is held by Prof. Cyrus Thomas that recent investigations prove they were the ancestors of the Shawnees. The latter were finally overwhelmed and scattered. Dr. D. G. Brinton, on the other hand, maintains that the ancestors of the Chatta-Muskogee tribes were probably the original mound building stock or family—these tribes embracing the Choctaws, Chickasaws, Natchez and other allied Southern Indians; for within the historic period, even, they were builders of earthworks and mound defenses. On this latter point Thruston, rightly regarded as an authority, says: "The widely-spread traditions of the Northern Indians, indicating that the race that built the imposing structures in the Ohio valley were driven to the southward, also favored this view; as does the fact that the mounds of Tennessee do not appear to be of so early a period as the Ohio mounds." But in the historic period the unknown land of Tennessee was marked on the new world maps as "the unexplored land of the ancient Shawnees."

There is no foundation, however, for the belief that the graves in some portions of the State indicate a race of pigmies. There are really no pigmy graves here.

One of the largest of the aboriginal cemeteries in the State lies about five miles south of Nashville on Brown's creek, between the Franklin and Middle Franklin turnpikes. Near this site there seems to have once been a large town. Not less than three thousand closely laid stone graves were found in the cemetery, and about a thousand more were found on nearby farms. In the central cemetery six or seven hundred perfect specimens of well-burned pottery were discovered; and nearly every familiar natural object is represented in the form of the ware—animals, birds, fish, the human figure and sea-shell forms. Many of the vessels have been colored and decorated with some artistic skill. In a child's grave of the ancient cemetery was a terra-cotta figure nine inches long, representing a papoose tied to its hanging board, which indicates that this modern Indian custom prevailed with the prehistoric tribes. Sets of toy plates, marbles, terra-cotta rattles, and crude tools and implements of pottery, stone and bone, were also unearthed.

It appears that in the immediate vicinity of Nashville no defensive works of any magnitude were erected; but a cordon of frontier forts, or fortified towns, protected this central and populous district.

STONE GRAVES.

The cists or box-shaped coffins are made of thin slabs of stone, sometimes broken or cut, and frequently rudely joined. The graves are six or seven feet long, a foot and a half or two feet wide, and eighteen inches deep; but graves of varying sizes are found. Frequently the cist contains two or three skeletons, and is not more than three or four feet long, indicating that they were probably interred long after death. Nearly all the graves are filled with earth inside, by infiltration. The roots of trees have penetrated them; the skulls are usually packed with earth. Vessels of pottery must have contained food and drink for the journey to the happy hunting ground, and are conveniently near the body. Graves exist on many of the large farms in central Tennessee within a radius of seventy-five miles of Nashville. In Wilson County, near Cottage Home— about fifty miles east of the capital—there are a large mound and cemetery. They are on the farm of the late Peter Clarke, situated about two hundred yards from the western bank of Smith Fork creek, and occupying three or four acres of ground. Mr. Leander Hays, a reliable gentleman who has lived on an adjoining farm since about 1835, said in 1899: "The mound fifty years ago was twenty-five feet above the level of the surrounding land, and nearby was a large basin, showing that the material was taken from that spot for the erection of the mound. There was a white oak tree on the mound's top, with rings indicating that it was three hundred years old. Some treasure-hunters made an excavation, digging a tunnel six feet in size. Portions of a skeleton, some pottery, and, if I recollect, a gunstock, were the only things discovered. There are traces of fortifications nearby, some portions being about four feet high fifty years ago. Within the space enclosed by this earth-work were a number of smaller mounds. A large number of graves in the fields bordering the creek were rock-lined, square, and contained skeletons in a sitting posture. Flint arrow-heads were numerous. At our old homestead, which I own now, there are two of these graves which have not been molested after discovered; one near the front gate, and the other in the garden, under an old apple tree."

Four miles east, on the same creek, in the bottom fields of the T. G. Bratton farm, Indian graves were once numerous, but have been destroyed by the plow-share. The bones were of a reddish tint, and crumbled when exposed to the air. They were in the vicinity of the trail referred to by Carr in his mention of the fight which took place between Winchester and the body of Indians under the leadership of the chief, the Moon.

A mile north of Liberty, on the farm of C. W. L. Hale, DeKalb County, there stands a large mound, evidently of artificial construction. The field in which it is seen has been under cultivation about seventy-five years, but the mound is yet of considerable dimensions, about fifteen feet high and a hundred feet in diameter. It was used perhaps as a place for observation by the Mound Builders, or for religious rites. Stone graves

A Prehistoric Giant. 159

were in close proximity. Across Smith Fork creek, a quarter of a mile from the mound, there was found a large grave in 1894 which caused considerable comment. It was very long, and the person buried there must have been of giant size. The jaw bone was said to have been large enough to slip with ease down over an adult's head. The Anakim were giants of importance in the early days in the Orient; David had a troop of giants; the emperor of Germany has shown partiality for a guard of men of large stature. No doubt the giant whose bones were unearthed in DeKalb County in 1894, where they had reposed for centuries, was a person of importance, stalking among his people conscious of their admiration, and when in battle witnessing with satisfaction the consternation his Goliath-like figure excited among his enemies.

Were the Cumberland settlements of the Mound Builders intended to be protected by the cordon of forts mentioned earlier in this chapter? There are ruins of fortifications in Sumner, Williamson and Wilson counties to indicate this. "Forts were probably not needed on the western and northwestern sides, already occupied by villages and settlements of the same race," suggests Thruston.

The works lying near Saundersville, Sumner County, inclose about fourteen acres. The earth lines and smaller mounds in the cultivated fields in 1897 were nearly obliterated, but in the woodland were well preserved. The chief mound near the center is nearly twenty-six feet high. It is about three hundred and eighteen feet in circumference, and is entirely artificial. The mounds next in size are composed probably of the debris of ancient houses. At irregular intervals along the earth lines in the woodland, angles of earth project about ten feet beyond the general line, indicating towers or bastions in the wall line.

There are also aboriginal works of interest at Castalian Springs, in the same county.

A fortified settlement is found on the Lindsley farm, east of Lebanon, containing about ten acres. The usual great mound is near the center. A large number of the smaller elevations proved to be the remains of dwelling houses or wigwams; when the earth was cleared away, hard, circular floors were disclosed, with burnt clay or ancient hearths in the center, indicating a similarity to the circular lodges of modern Indians. From beneath the floors—many of the Indians buried their dead under their dwellings—were taken some of the finest specimens of pottery and ancient art yet discovered in mounds.

On the southwest bank of the Big Harpeth river, in Williamson County, on the De Graffenreid farm, about two and a half miles from Franklin, and twenty miles south of Nashville, vestiges of the ditch and embankment of a fortified settlement are visible, though the land has been tilled for nearly a century. The enclosure contains about thirty-two acres of land. The earthwork is a crescent or semi-circle, 3,800 feet in length, and the ends resting on an impassable, almost perpendicular bluff of the river, rising about forty feet from the water's edge. The land is unusually fertile within the enclosure, and the water is convenient and inexhaustible. The place would have maintained a protracted siege. There are nine mounds within the earthworks; the largest is two hundred and thirty feet in length, one hundred and ten feet in breadth, and sixteen feet in height. The mounds and ditch were covered with trees. A white oak four feet in diameter stood in the ditch. In one of the mounds was a skeleton in a sitting posture. Within the bones of the hand was held a flint knife or sword blade, the fingers resting around the tapering end or handle. The instrument was twenty-two inches long, and two inches wide at the broadest portion. It is said to be the longest and finest chipped stone knife known to archæology. An earthenware vessel was on the left side, as if held in the hand, and two large sea-shells lay on the right. In other graves there were some small, thin copper plates, stamped with rude crosses; also, unique images and fine specimens of painted pottery and of shell work.

There are also mounds and groups of mounds in Maury County, in the Sequatchee valley, on Caney Fork, and in Madison and Lawrence counties. On the east side of the Tennessee river, on the high ground adjoining the town of Savannah, there are extensive earthworks. But the largest and most elaborate ancient fortification in Middle Tennessee is situated in the forks of Duck river, near Manchester in Coffee County. In 1897 the main wall varied from four to six feet in height. It is partly constructed of irregular, loose stone from the river bed or the adjoining bluffs. There is no regular wall or masonry, but the rocks and earth are heaped together promiscuously, forming a strong embankment, connecting with the steep river bluffs. A wide, deep ditch in the rear of the works separates and protects them from the commanding ridge opposite. The entrance at the north end exhibits considerable engineering skill, and is similar in plan to some of the fortified gateways of the strongest ancient works in Ohio. Mounds of stone about three feet higher than the general wall—doubtless foundations for lower or extra defenses—were erected on each side of the entrance. On the inside, double protecting walls extend back from the opening, terminating at both ends in raised mounds of the same character, opposite the main entrance and rear opening, the latter being concealed at the side. "The enemy once within the main gateway, would find himself in a *cul de sac* in this enclosure." Explorations made have revealed no stone graves or other remains of interest, or connecting it with aboriginal life in other fortified works. The stone fort is supposed to have been a military enclosure, not used as a permanent settlement.

When lived the people to whom we give the name of Mound Builders for the lack of a more appropriate

MERE SPECULATIONS. 163

one? From the excellent state of preservation of many of the skeletons, shell, bone and horn ornaments and implements, sun-dried pottery, and articles of wood, found in some of the mounds and stone graves of Middle Tennessee, Thruston contends that it cannot be believed that all of the latter ante-dated the discovery of this country by Columbus, the visit of Pamphilo De Narvaez in 1728, or of De Soto in 1540.

But the mystery surrounding the prehistoric race or races of Tennessee will in all probability never be satisfactorily explained. The centuries keep no records, and where man has failed to do so, speculation and wonder are all that are left.

> "Sages and chiefs long since had birth
>   Ere Caesar was, or Newton named;
> Those raised new empires o'er the earth,
>   And these new heavens and systems named;
> Vain was the chief's, the sage's pride—
> They had no poet, and they died!"

sang Pope; and the lack of the poet and historian is painfully felt in the especial case of the aboriginal races of America.

CHAPTER XVI.

THE BATTLE OF KING'S MOUNTAIN, AND TENNESSEE'S CONNECTION WITH THE REVOLUTION.

The battle of King's Mountain was not fought on Tennessee soil, but as Tennesseans were engaged in it, it has an additional historic interest to citizens of this State.

The first counties organized in what afterwards became Tennessee were Washington, organized in November, 1777, and Sullivan, taken from Washington in 1779 and named for Gen. Sullivan. John Sevier held the position of colonel-commandant of the first, and Isaac Shelby that of the second. Sevier has been mentioned. Shelby was another of those daring Indian fighters whose courage contributed to the success of the early settlements.

In 1780 the revolutionary cause in the South seemed on the point of collapsing. Charleston fell, Gen. Gates had been defeated, Gen. Sumter had met with reverses. Only a few partisans kept the spirit of the colonists alive. Lord Cornwallis by September had been reinforced by about three thousand men from Clinton's command at New York, and passed triumphantly into North Carolina; Patrick Ferguson, with a command of regulars and tories, moving on his left, was threatening

THE PATRIOTS AROUSED. 165

the western frontiers with fire and sword; and many patriots submitted to British authority, considering their freedom lost.

But a turning point came at last. The threats of Ferguson had aroused the frontiersmen, and gathering under Sevier and Shelby, they brought about one of the most brilliant victories of the war, at King's Mountain, N. C., made the American republic a certainty, and, as Phelan correctly observes, connected the history of Tennessee with Bunker Hill and the ancient history of the United States. They resolved to arrest the brilliant British officer's progress, and soon had him on the retreat and writing to Lord Cornwallis for assistance against those he had but a few days before threatened.

Shelby dispatched a messenger to Col. William Campbell on the Holston; and the field officers of Southwestern Virginia invited him with four hundred men to join in the expedition against Ferguson. An express was also sent to Col. Cleaveland, of North Carolina. All were to meet and unite, and accordingly on September 25, 1780, the three regiments under Campbell, Sevier and Shelby, and some North Carolina fugitives under McDowell, assembled on the Watauga to begin their march.

Five days afterwards they formed a junction with the regiment of Col. Cleaveland. Their advance startled the enemy. "A numerous army now appeared on the frontier drawn from Nollichucky and other settlements beyond the mountains, whose very names had been unknown to us," wrote Lord Rawdon later, and the missive tends to show the trepidation the few hundred men put the British in. But when the vigor of movement and the personal appearance of those hardy mountaineers are considered, it is hardly a matter for wonder that they were magnified into a "numerous army." We can in imagination see the consternation of the Grecians when Alaric the Goth appeared on their borders, and realize something of the fierce appearance of Attila's horde of Huns as they advanced on Italy. The American riflemen, though insignificant in numbers compared with those old-world legions, were as picturesque and terrorizing in their appearance; and they were actuated by patriotism and not plunder as they issued from the mountain fastnesses, and this made them all the more formidable. Not a bayonet was amongst them; but few swords dangled at their officers' sides; not a tent was carried to protect them from the cold autumn nights. But their fringed and tasseled hunting shirts were girded in by bead-worked belts, and the trappings of their horses were stained red and yellow. On their heads they wore coon-skin or mink-skin caps, with the tails hanging down, or else felt hats in each of which was thrust a buck tail or a sprig of green. All carried small-bore rifles, tomahawks and scalping knives. Before leaving on the march, they had assembled in a grove and heard Rev. Samuel Doak invoke the blessings of Heaven on the expedition; and the light of a just cause shone in their eyes and on their rough and scarred and weather-beaten countenances. Then their commanders —these were the embodiment of valor and determination also. There was Campbell, brave and watchful; Shelby, with his iron nerves and the fearless and audacious look which comes of frequent and victorious encounters with death; Sevier, with his knightly bearing, who though only thirty-five years of age, had his two gallant sons there to watch over; McDowell and Williams, eager and alert; and, lastly, Cleaveland, a Hercules in size and anxious to avenge the wrongs the loyalists had inflicted on him and his people. What champions to keep "the lamp of chivalry alight in hearts of gold!"

After a few days this "numerous army" of less than fifteen hundred men reached the Cowpens on Broad river. Here they held a council of war and it was decided to start that night to strike the British by surprise; for this enterprise they picked out nine hundred and ten of their best horsemen, all expert marksmen; and at eight o'clock the same evening the selected men began their march. On the afternoon of October 7 they were at the foot of King's Mountain, on the top of which Ferguson, with eleven hundred and twenty-five men—one hundred and twenty-five of them regulars—were camped, confident that he could not be beaten.

The Americans dismounted, and formed themselves into four columns. A part of Cleveland's regiment, headed by Winston, and Sevier's regiment, formed a column on the right. The other part of Cleaveland's regiment, headed by that partisan himself, and the regiment of Williams, composed the left wing. The post of extreme danger was assigned to the column formed by Campbell's regiment on the right center, and Shelby's regiment on the left center; so that Sevier's right nearly adjoined Shelby's left. The right and left wings were to pass the position of Ferguson, and from opposite sides climb the ridge, fortified by nature with slate-cliffs forming breastworks, in his rear; while the two central columns were to attack in front. In this order they advanced to within a quarter of a mile of the British before discovered.

The two center columns, headed by Campbell and Shelby, climbing the mountain, began the attack. Shelby went on up. The enemy's regulars charged Campbell with fixed bayonets; and his riflemen, having no bayonets, gave way for a short distance only, and then returned with additional ardor. The two columns with some aid from a part of Sevier's regiment, kept up a furious battle with Ferguson's force for ten minutes; then the right and left wings of the Americans advanced upon the British flank and rear; the fire became general; for fifty-five minutes longer the volleying was incessant. At last the American right wing gained the top of the mountain, and the British—Ferguson being killed—attempted to retreat along the top of the ridge. They were held in check by Williams and Cleaveland, and Capt. De Peyster hoisted a white flag. The firing ceased soon, and the enemy surrendered at discretion.

RESULT OF THE VICTORY. 169

The loss of the British was eleven hundred and four —the number of prisoners was six hundred and forty-eight, according to Bancroft. The Americans' loss was twenty-eight killed and sixty wounded.

Gregg, an English historian, says: "Of some six hundred and fifty captives, a number were hanged in cold blood on the next morning, under the eyes of the American commander."

But the whole truth is, that among the captives were house-burners and assassins; and private soldiers who had witnessed the sorrows of helpless women and children, executed nine or ten of these creatures—"for the frequent use of the gallows at Camden, Ninety-Six, and Augusta," as Bancroft explains; but Col. Campbell intervened and prevented further delinquences.

"The victory at King's Mountain, which in the spirit of the American soldiers was like the rising at Concord, in its effects like the successes at Bennington, changed the aspect of the war," observes Bancroft. "The victory," declares Roosevelt, "was of far-reaching importance, and ranks among the decisive battles of the Revolution. It was the first great success of the Americans in the South, the turning point in the Southern campaign, and it brought cheer to the patriots throughout the Union."

A sword and a pair of pistols were voted to Sevier and Shelby by the General Assembly of North Carolina, which debt of gratitude was not paid till 1810. The soldiers received liquidated certificates worth two cents on the dollar for their services. Shelby's share of these for services in 1780-81 was sold by him for "six yards of middling broadcloth." But they were not fighting for lucre. Both Sevier and Shelby, after a war with the Indians for the protection of the frontiers, joined Marion with Washington and Sullivan county men, in behalf of independence.

CHAPTER XVII.

THE STORY OF CONSTITUTION MAKING, FROM THE WATAUGA ASSOCIATION TO 1800.

The Anglo-Saxon race from an early day has had great faith in a fundamental political structure called the constitution, and reverence it as the bulwark of their liberties. This was made manifest west of the Alleghenies in the action of the Wataugans in 1772. The line between Virginia and North Carolina was run in 1771, and they found their settlements in the latter colony, and not in Virginia, as they had supposed, and separated from the parent colony by distance and almost impassable ranges of mountains. The affairs of North Carolina were disordered, and the Western settlers could expect no aid or protection from her, and they hoped for none from the general government. They found themselves without government, although the community was already infested to some extent by lawless characters who had come with the wave of immigration. Watauga was in an anomalous position, it can be seen. "For government," says Bancroft, "its members in 1772 came together as brothers in convention, and founded a republic by a written association; appointed their own magistrates, Robertson among the first; framed laws for their present occasions; and set to the people of America the example of erecting themselves into a State, independent of the British king." Perhaps they hardly intended such independence as the distinguished historian suggests, but Watauga was the first free independent community established by men of American birth on this continent.

The constitution of Watauga has perished, and we know very little of the contents of the instrument; but it is thought that the Cumberland compact, made later by persons who were identified with the Watauga movement and preserved in part, is in many respects a reproduction of it. Thirteen commissioners were elected— John Carter, Charles Robertson, Zach Isbell, John Sevier, James Smith, James Robertson, Jacob Brown, William Bean, John Jones, George Russell, Jacob Womack, Robert Lucas and William Tatham. Of these John Carter, Charles and James Robertson, Zack Isbell and John Sevier were selected as a court, or board of five commissioners, and William Tatham made clerk. The settlements originally composing the association were Watauga and Carter's Valley, but the Nollichucky, or Brown settlement, was admitted later. The principle of representation appears to have been fairly employed, for in the subsequent petition to be annexed to North Carolina it was declared that the committee had been chosen unanimously by consent of the people, and had acted with the consent of every individual. The Wataugans were mostly from North Carolina and Virginia, and the settlers of these colonies were largely

English. Ninety-eight per cent of the white Virginian population were English. This assured Anglo-Saxon blood and principles in the little commonwealth. The fundamental tenets of this association were therefore Anglo-Saxon—personal liberty and representative government, from all that can be gathered; and this should satisfy our curiosity relative to the movement which has assumed an undue conspicuousness in history.

Robertson, Isbell, Lucas and Tatham went a few years later and settled on the Cumberland; and so in 1780, when the settlements there had grown, and the representatives of seven stations met in Nashborough on May 1, they must have exerted an influence in the making of the constitution framed by this convention. The compact, excepting the first page, has been preserved, with certain amendments made on May 13. Two hundred and fifty-six persons signed it; and though the instrument contains a recognition of the fact that the Cumberland settlement belonged to North Carolina, that settlement really became another State founded upon the consent of the governed. The reasons given for its organization are thought to represent the purposes of the Watauga settlers. Was not the wording borrowed from the older compact? Instead of a committee of thirteen, however, it provided for a committee of twelve, and they are referred to as the judges, triers, or general arbitrators. The sub-committee of five do not appear to have been retained, either; for the judges or triers are declared to have the proper jurisdiction for the recovery of debt or damage, provided the cause of action had arisen among the settlers when they were beyond the limits of government. Cases involving one hundred dollars or less were tried before three judges, whose decision was final. If the amount was larger, an appeal could be taken to the twelve—or rather to nine—of the committee, for the three from whose judgment an appeal was taken were excluded. The judges had criminal jurisdiction, but were forbidden to proceed with execution "so far as to effect life or member," in which case the offender was to be sent under guard to the place where the offense had been committed, or to a place where a legal trial could be had—perhaps in the older section of North Carolina.

The Cumberland institutions were thoroughly English, like those of Watauga. In April, 1783, the Legislature of North Carolina created Davidson county, and the compact of the Cumberland settlements became obsolete.

As shown in a previous chapter, the State of Franklin was organized in the Eastern section under the leadership of Sevier in 1784, and collapsed four years subsequently. When the scheme to form it materialized, the North Carolina constitution, with some immaterial modifications, was adopted at the suggestion of Sevier. That constitution was, according to competent critics, a democratic, a thoroughly American, version of the English constitution.

ENUMERATION OF INHABITANTS. 175

In this connection it may be instructive to show that the Legislature of Franklin appointed Sevier governor and made other necessary officers in the spring of 1785; and amusing to note the Solons grappling with a financial system. "In addition to the ordinary medium of exchange," says Caldwell in his constitutional history, "divers commodities were made legal tender. Tow linen, for instance, was legal tender at the rate of one shilling nine pence a yard, and linsey at three shillings; clean beaver skins, six shillings each; raccoon and fox skins, one shilling and three pence; bacon and tallow, six pence a pound; rye whiskey, two shillings and six pence a gallon; peach and apple brandy, three shillings a gallon; maple sugar, one shilling a pound. Thus the governor might have been compelled to take the amount of his salary in bees-wax and rye whiskey!"

The territorial organization, having been entirely artificial, will not be noticed here.

On July 11, 1795, the Territorial Assembly passed an act for the enumeration of the inhabitants of the territory of Tennessee with the view of creating a new State. The enumeration indicated the population as being 77,262, of whom 10,613 were slaves, and 973 were distinguished as "other free persons." More than a third of all the voters of the territory opposed a State government.

The constitutional convention was called and assembled at Knoxville on July 11, 1796. There were then eleven counties—Blount, Davidson, Greene, Hawkins,

Jefferson, Knox, Sullivan, Sevier, Sumner, Tennessee and Washington. The members of the convention numbered fifty-five. It was opened with prayer, and by a sermon by Rev. Samuel Carrick. William Blount, territorial governor, was president. The committee appointed to draft the constitution was composed of Andrew Jackson, John McNairy, Samuel Frazier, William Rankin, William Cocke, Thomas Henderson, Joseph Anderson, James Roddey, William Blount, Charles McClung, W. C. C. Claiborne, John Rhea, David Shelby, Daniel Smith, Samuel Wear, John Clack, Thomas Johnston, William Fort, John Tipton and James Stewart.

Like the Franklin people, Tennessee virtually adopted the North Carolina constitution—a constitution at once democratic and conservative in method.

The first place was given to the Legislature, and too much power was vested in that department. One senator and two representatives were provided from each county in the first Assembly, but after the census which was to be taken within three years of the first meeting of Assembly, senators and representatives were to be apportioned according to the number of taxable inhabitants, not according to population. Was not here a property qualification? And no one could be a member who had not for one year possessed and continued to possess two hundred acres of land. The body was to fix all salaries, though until 1804 these were paid:

To the governor, $750.

To the judges, not more than $600.

A Study in Salaries.

To the secretary, not over $400.

To the treasurer or treasurers, not more than four per cent for receiving and paying out all funds.

To the attorney or attorneys, not over $50 for each court attended.

Land, excepting town lots, was to be taxed uniformly, and lots were not to be assessed higher than two hundred acres of land.

There was a poll-tax on slaves, not to be more than the tax on two hundred acres of land.

The governor was elected by the people for a term of two years, was to be twenty-five years of age and to own five hundred acres of land. His successor in case of death, resignation, etc., was the speaker of the senate.

Every free-holder over the age of twenty-one, and every male citizen over that age who had been for six months a resident of the county where his vote was offered, was an elector of the governor and members of the General Assembly. Even free negroes voted, and continued to do so until the constitution of 1834.

The judicial power was invested in such superior and inferior courts of law and equity as the Legislature might establish.

The judges and attorneys general were elected by joint ballot of the two houses, to hold office during good behavior.

Each court appointed its own clerk, to hold his office during good behavior.

Magistrates were appointed by the General Assembly, and commissioned by the governor. They were also to hold during good behavior; their number not to exceed two for each captain's company (of militia), except that the company which included the county seat was entitled to three.

Coroners, trustees and constables were elected by the county court for two years; rangers and registers were appointed by that tribunal also, to serve during good behavior.

There were no civil districts until 1834.

It was not necessary for legislative action to call out the militia.

Clergymen were denied the right to sit in the Assembly.

No one who denied the being of God or a future state of rewards and punishments was allowed to hold any office in the civil department of the State, but he might in the military.

Persons could be imprisoned for debt, unless the debtors should surrender their estate for the benefit of creditors, where the presumption of fraud was not strong.

The press was to be free, and the principles of the English and American Bills of Rights were declared to be essential parts of the constitution.

As to religious liberty it was declared: "That all men have a natural and indefeasible right to worship Almighty God according to the dictates of their own consciences; that no man can of right be compelled to attend, erect, or support any place of worship, or to maintain any ministry against his consent; that no human authority can in any case whatever control or interfere with the rights of conscience; and that no preference shall ever be given by law to any religious establishment or mode of worship. That no religious test shall ever be required as a qualification to any office or public trust under this State."

The constitution was said by Thomas Jefferson—one of whose great hobbies was religious liberty—to be the least imperfect and most republican of the State constitutions. However, it contained grave defects, which have since been remedied to some extent. These changes may be noted by a comparison of it with the present State constitution.

In 1796 the State contained three districts—Washington, Mero, and Hamilton. On August 8 of that year an act was passed naming three persons from each county to choose the presidential electors. The commissioners so chosen from the counties of Washington district were to meet at Jonesboro, those from Mero at Nashville, and those from Hamilton at Knoxville, on a day designated, and ballot for electors for their respective districts. In case of a tie, the decision was to be made by drawing lots. This unique method no longer prevails, and the Presidential electors are chosen by the people at a regular election.

CHRONOLOGICAL TABLE.

First Settlement in Tennessee, at Watauga	1768
Watauga Association Formed	1772
Indians, Through British Agents, Seek to Destroy East Tennessee Settlements	1776
First Settlement in Middle Tennessee	1778
Jonesboro, the First Town on Tennessee Soil, Laid Off	1779
First Literary School, Established by Samuel Doak	1780
John Sevier Takes Part in Battle of King's Mountain	1780
North Carolina Cedes Her Western Settlements	1784
Cession Act Repealed	1785
State of Franklin Formed	1785
End of the State of Franklin	1788
Tennessee Ceded by North Carolina	1790
Tennessee Becomes a Territory	1790
Indians Begin to Migrate	1790
First Federal Census of the Territory	1790
First Tennessee Newspaper, Founded at Rogersville	1791
Knoxville Laid Off	1792
John Sevier's Last Military Service	1793
Nickojack Expedition, from Nashville	1794
Tennessee Admitted to the Union	1796
John Sevier Elected Governor for the First Term	1796
First General Assembly Meets at Knoxville	1796
Andrew Jackson Elected to Congress	1796
William Blount and William Cocke Elected United States Senators	1796
Senator Blount expelled from the United States Senate	1797

AUTHORITIES CITED.

CIVIL AND POLITICAL HISTORY OF THE STATE OF TENNESSEE, from Its First Settlement up to the Year 1796. By John Haywood. 1823.

EARLY TIMES IN MIDDLE TENNESSEE. By John Carr. 1857.

HISTORY OF MIDDLE TENNESSEE; OR, LIFE AND TIMES OF GEN. JAMES ROBERTSON. By A. W. Putnam. 1859.

ANNALS OF TENNESSEE TO THE END OF THE EIGHTEENTH CENTURY. By J. G. M. Ramsey. 1860.

HISTORY OF TENNESSEE; THE MAKING OF A STATE. By James Phelan. 1888.

HISTORY OF THE CUMBERLAND PRESBYTERIAN CHURCH. By B. W. McDonnold. 1888.

CONSTITUTIONAL STUDIES IN TENNESSEE HISTORY. By Joshua Caldwell. 1895.

ANTIQUITIES OF TENNESSEE AND THE ADJACENT STATES. By Gates P. Thruston. 1897.

DROPPED STITCHES IN TENNESSEE HISTORY. By John Allison. 1897.

LIFE OF J. D. GOODPASTURE. By A. V. and W. H. Goodpasture. 1898.

www.ingramcontent.com/pod-product-compliance
Lightning Source LLC
Chambersburg PA
CBHW071423160426
43195CB00013B/1788